A Young Widow's Journey

Through Brokenness and Back

believe

D1403555

JENNIFER SILVERA

Kregel
Publications

Cover photographs of the author and her children taken by Lisa Slotsve (http://www.lisaslotsvephotography.com) and edited by Jose Charriez.

Library of Congress Cataloging-in-Publication Data
Silvera, Jennifer.
Believe : a young widow's journey through brokenness and back / Jennifer Silvera.
    p. cm.
1. Widows—Religious life. 2. Death—Religious aspects—Christianity.
3. Bereavement—Religious aspects—Christianity. 4. Grief—Religious aspects—Christianity. I. Title.
BV4528.S55   2009   248.8'66092—dc22[B]   2009002510

ISBN 978-0-8254-3657-4

Printed in the United States of America
09 10 11 12 13 / 5 4 3 2 1

For Jordan and Madelynn—
I believe in many great things for you.
And so did Daddy.

Anything is possible if you believe.

"What do you mean, 'If I can'?" Jesus asked.
"Anything is possible if a person believes."
The father instantly cried out,
"I do believe, but help me overcome my unbelief!"

MARK 9:23–24 NLT

If I wish to create, where do I start?
I will start with the truest love I've known,
and the truest love I've given.
This is the love that changed me.
This is the love that heals me.
This is the love that beckons me to believe.

—J. SILVERA

Contents

The Moment That Changes Everything

*If I could sing to you, I would sing with my best voice.
If I could hold your hand, I know I would feel stronger.
If I could see the smile in your eyes, I would feel like I was
seventeen again, meeting you for the first time. Then we
could start our journey all over.*

—JENNIFER'S JOURNAL
September 8, 2005

Darkness doesn't announce when it will knock on the door. It doesn't ask permission to enter. We're given little preparation for it, and we can't hide from it. Some darkness in life is almost too heavy to bear, sinking us into deep waters, almost like drowning.

Still, we fight for breath against disbelief. And in each moment, we struggle to find significance amid loss. Out of pure survival, we begin the pursuit of meaning and contentment for what remains of our lives. And, indeed, that pursuit has the power to hold great worth. Because on the road between darkness and contentment lies a mystery—the story that traces the journey. And every story of loss, every journey down that difficult road, has the potential not only to help the traveler reach meaning but to help others traveling along the way reach meaning as well.

I never asked for darkness to enter my life. But it came. I wasn't given a choice. No warning. Uninvited, like a malicious disease taking up residence in my body, in a single moment, hardship and struggle spread furiously into my contented world. The mixture of grief, loss, and brutal pain penetrated into every corner of who I was—a darkness I couldn't comprehend. I wanted to deny its claim on me, ignore the life-threatening report, find a cure, jump into the water and let it take me too.

Through pure will to survive—or complete madness, or simply not knowing what else to do—I found myself forced to study this thing called grief. I made a commitment. I would dissect my journey through loss. Writing became my vessel, my passageway to life again.

Some may mistake my way through darkness as endurance—a therapy, a coping mechanism. Knowing that my loss would always follow me, my journey was actually created to discover hope. Most likely what I thought was my own determination was really God graciously walking with me in my search, so that one day if I could find his hope, I would sing.

I would sing with my best voice.

PART ONE

LOSS

God bless this night
keep us safe
protect our hearts
when we are far away

Guide us, keep us
in care and grace
love us, help us
through each waking day

PRAYER FROM HONDURAS JOURNAL
June 21, 2002

CHAPTER I

Our Last Day

Love knows no limit to its endurance, no end to its trust,
no fading of its hope; it can outlast anything. It is, in fact,
the one thing that still stands when all else has fallen.

—1 CORINTHIANS 13:7–8 PHILLIPS

That day, all the windows in the house were open to capture the last smells and sounds of an Indian summer. From a distance, other noises floated in—the animated voices of children, the hum of cars passing through the residential maze, the neighbor's air conditioner. Inside the radio was turned down low, the announcer making some comment about the heat. I had just returned home from a quick errand to drop film off at the store to be developed.

The warm weather indeed seemed out of place for September. It felt more like the middle of summer instead of the first day of school—a perfect day to be lazy, though that wasn't an option since my husband had only fifteen minutes before he needed to be at work. We were just finishing a big lunch of homemade mushroom ravioli and tossed salad—really more like dinner, due to a police officer's schedule—when with a quick glance of the clock, Shawn jumped up to put his plate in the dishwasher.

"I can get that," I said, trying to save him time as he started getting ready to leave for his afternoon shift.

"I got it," he replied and hurried to grab his thermos of coffee, extra cream.

"Shawn, I'm overwhelmed," I told him. I knew this wasn't the time to start a long conversation, but sometimes parenthood doesn't allow opportune moments.

"With what?" he asked not looking up, but still trying to show attention.

"With being a mom," I started. "I don't think I'm very good at it. It's harder than I ever thought, Shawn. I want to stay at home with our kids but I didn't know it would be like this. I think I'm better at human resources with an office and an assistant and a cell phone. I'm constantly exhausted."

He laughed and then stopped to look me in the eyes. "We're going to figure this out, Jen. This parent thing. We can do it. I tell you what; I have four days off starting tomorrow. You plan all four days. Whatever you want to do. If you need time alone or have things you want us to do together—organize each day and you can tell me the plan tonight."

I smiled at the deal. Even my old office perks couldn't beat that. It felt good to be heard. It felt reassuring to be in our roles of parenthood *together*.

Glancing at his watch he ended the discussion, "Gotta run."

He kissed me with car keys clutched in one hand, a lunch cooler in the other, and his work bag strapped on his shoulder. Hair still wet from his shower, he was dressed in street clothes. He always changed into his uniform at work, claimed this was more efficient—if we were out or if there were an emergency, he could go straight to the department without needing to stop home first. It was his way of planning ahead.

He looked good. He looked more than good. I didn't want him to leave. But it was 1:51 PM, and I'd already made him late.

As he backed down the driveway, I ran out of the house. "Wait! Shawn! Wait!" I shouted, waving him back. "I forgot to give you your card."

"Thanks," he said, grabbing the envelope through the open window. Love notes in his lunch box were my trademark.

"Hey . . . do you even like these notes I send with you?" I asked, knowing he had to hurry.

"Yeah, they're nice," he told me.

Although he was in a rush, his answer wasn't enough for me. "Shawn, if you don't like these notes, I don't have to keep sending them with you."

"I like the notes, Jen," he said with a bit of indifference, but giving me a grin.

"Okay, then. Open it at work," I told him. "It's from me and the kids."

"Okay, gotta go—for real," he said with one last smile—now in a more obvious hurry. He tucked the note in the side of his work bag and sped off.

I stood in the driveway with Jordan balanced on my hip. Our little boy waved an extra long time until his daddy's car was out of sight. He waited, eager to click the automatic garage door button as part of our routine. With the door shut, we walked upstairs to find Madelynn cooing in her baby swing.

It was a normal sort of day—wave goodbye and smile, we love you.

Inside our house the radio still hummed. It was nap time, my treasured two-hour block of sanity. I hurried to put the kids down for a nap and then changed into shorts and a tank top to exercise on our elliptical machine. I needed to get back into shape from having babies . . . and I also needed to adjust my attitude on motherhood. Exercise is good for keeping things in perspective.

After my workout, I pulled out a pile of photo albums and spread them across the kitchen table. I began to assemble the books with Shawn's photography; it was his new hobby—a developing talent that had slowly been turning into a side job of baby portraits and even a handful of weddings. The work of artistically arranging the photos into proof books for clients was a creative outlet for me.

It wasn't long before the kids were waking up with lots of energy for the afternoon. I debated whether to begin the routine of supper early or stall the process with a stroller ride around the block.

Then the doorbell rang.

Not dressed for company, I quickly threw a T-shirt over my tank before running to greet our unexpected visitors.

"Ringing?" Jordan asked with enthusiasm.

"Yes, that's the doorbell. Let's go see who it is!" I responded, my voice tinged with playful intrigue. Sometimes a surprise distraction in the middle of the day is a nice diversion for a stay-at-home mom.

Standing at the top of the steps of our new split-level home, I tilted my head to look through the side windows in the entryway. A trio of silhouettes dressed in dark colors stood on the front porch. I was perplexed. *How odd for three men to show up at our house in the late afternoon,* I thought. *Who could they be?* My mind began searching for possibilities.

Maybe they were neighbors coming to ask Shawn about setting up for next weekend's block party. Perhaps they were selling something? Or soliciting donations? Following my natural instinct to offer a warm, Midwestern welcome, I raced to open the door.

Three uniformed police officers stood, unmoving, visibly distressed.

Even without words, I knew. Their presence, their expressions conveyed the message. I knew deep down that Shawn was dead. And I wanted to shut my door and run back up the stairs to the life I'd known only seconds before. I had two babies waiting for a stroller ride and dinner to make. Why did they come and change that?

The Chief of Police spoke first. "There's been an accident, Jennifer . . . Shawn . . . Shawn's been killed." His words fumbled apologetically.

Surely I'd misheard him.

Another voice asked, "Can we take you upstairs?"

I didn't understand. Nothing made sense. I was beginning to fade. My mind struggled to make connections. Shock threatened to overcome me. They ushered me upstairs to the living room.

Yet another voice said, "Let us help you sit down."

Sit down? How would that help? I shook my head, refusing, "No . . . no . . . no . . ."

"We'll need to make some phone calls. Who should we call first?" asked one of them. I recognized him as a sergeant who worked with Shawn at the police department.

I sank, legs tucked underneath me, to the floor, muttering, "I can't believe this. I can't believe this."

I kept thinking, *We're not prepared for this. Shawn, we're not prepared. I don't know who to call. I don't have a phone list for this type of situation. You can't be dead because I don't know how to do this.*

"Jennifer," said the voice again. "Jennifer . . . it's me, Sergeant Bill. Should we call Shawn's mom?"

"Yes," I replied, like I knew the protocol for what to do when your husband dies. "Wait! No! You can't call her. She's home alone. She can't get this message by herself."

My brain was fighting between being rational and becoming numb. Shawn's father had died a year and a half earlier, and I panicked at the thought of Bonnie, alone, learning that her son had been killed.

"We can send a squad car to her home," Sergeant Bill told me. "Who do you want to call? Shawn's brother? Sister? Your family? We can also send a squad car to your parents' home."

My fingers covered my lips, and my breath felt cold inside my hands. I felt like I was going to throw up. I ran my fingers through my hair and held my temples. My body was shaking and I felt lightheaded.

Why were they asking me to decide this? I didn't want to call anyone. I didn't want this to be true, and if we made even that first phone call, weren't we admitting to the nightmare?

Where were my kids? I glanced around to find them. In the corner of the living room, Jordan was using one-word sentences to teach one of the officers how to use our vacuum cleaner. This same officer was holding Madelynn, who was babbling happily. My children were at ease. The officer took them downstairs to play in the basement Shawn had just finished. That was *his* basement! His handiwork and labor. He needed to be here!

The chief was standing by our kitchen patio door, peering at the open space below. There wasn't a deck yet. Shawn had planned to start building one the following summer. Uncomfortable, he turned around and told me, "Jennifer, Sergeant Bill will stay with you to help. I need to go back to the accident site. We're here for you. For whatever you need. Just tell Bill and we'll make it happen."

Then the chief was gone and Sergeant Bill patiently explained to me again the importance of contacting family. "Jennifer, we need to get your family here, and then we can take everyone to the ambulance to see Shawn," he said. "If that's what you want. We don't think you should go alone."

"Call his brother, Mark, and sister, Nicole, and then my sister Deanna," I decided. I trusted my sister would tell me what to do. She was calm and able to think under pressure. My mind was failing me, and I needed someone strong.

I felt my mind drawing me to a place I'd never been. I didn't know where I was being taken, and I didn't want to follow into the unknown. Scarier still, I realized that I had no choice. My spirit was falling into a cave carved by darkness. Not knowing what else to do, my body gave up and followed.

If I could hold your hand, I know I would feel stronger.

I went into a trancelike state, rocking, holding my face in my hands. I wanted to tell the officers in my house—none of whom I knew very well—that this couldn't be happening. But they couldn't hear my swirling thoughts because I couldn't speak.

I knew they were speaking words, but the more they said, the less I heard. With each question, I felt I was losing my capacity to understand. The sounds collided into a mass of deafening noise. I couldn't think. Everything inside of me turned off. The safety of shock set in.

I began to ignore these strangers in my house and got up to put away the photo albums. I couldn't stay sitting on the floor.

"Jennifer, you don't need to do that," one of them said.

I couldn't even mumble a response. *Please let me clean,* I begged with my eyes as the officers stared at me. *Please let me put something back in order,* my heart was pleading.

I grabbed a Kleenex box from the bathroom and threw it on the coffee table, trying to take some type of control amidst the devastation. I knew people would soon be arriving, crying, looking for a tissue. My husband had just died, and I was making sure the house was presentable. An absurd defense mechanism. All the while, my whole body begged for the return of normal.

My forced activity was a cover. Internally, I'd entered a most hollow place. I'd spilled into a cold, dark hole, spiraling farther and farther from light. The light was the life I'd known, the life created with my husband, the very best part of me. The message that he was gone tolled inside my mind, over and over, like a chant. Yet I couldn't fully grasp it. Why was this happening to me?

I slipped farther into a void between life and death, a place I hadn't known existed. This was my initiation into a comatoselike existence.

People began to arrive. Spinning. The room was spinning and changing shape. Our picture on the wall above the couch seemed out of place. It was an oil painting on canvas of a garden scene with an open gate, a present from Shawn for my birthday. I stared at the image blurring in front of me wishing I could walk inside it, down the garden path and go find him.

Everything looked out of place—the strangers in my house. The family in my house. The Kleenex on the coffee table. *That's not where we keep the tissue box. Is this where I live?*

My vision faded in and out, thoughts crashing inside my head. My only coherent thoughts were framed in fear or doubt. I wanted to scream, "Give me my life back. Leave my house. Take this news to someone else. I don't understand. Don't take my life away!"

I was a prisoner being transported against my will to a foreign land. This new territory brought new sights that I didn't want to see or experience or even know about. Nothing here made sense. I was a stranger inside my own life, trapped in a place of anguish, without guidance of how to return home. Extremely weak and ill-prepared for the journey, my entire being filled with panic. How could I know the way home from a place I'd never been? Shawn had been my compass. Where does one go when one is lost?

For the first time, life felt undeniably cruel.

Looking back, I can retrace every step in my mind as if in slow motion. One small turn of my wrist to open the door, three silhouetted figures. On one side of the door lived normalcy, on the other side destruction waited. What would have happened had I kept the door shut? Illogical. Impossible. But still I imagine. Could I have prevented, ignored, or even denied the news? Why didn't I have a choice?

Have you ever had such an experience? Wished you could replay time? Thought, "If only I'd done something differently, I may have been able to change what happened within that moment."

I had so many "what-ifs." I thought, *What if I'd asked Shawn to stay home from work that day? Would he have listened? Would Shawn still be alive?* The questions only perpetuated my madness. I was already teetering along the line of insanity, and these kinds of thoughts only added to the crazy-making.

Within twenty-four hours of Shawn's death, I was kneeling on my bedroom floor, arms raised toward heaven, in a mess of tears, begging God to prove to me that he was there. "God, are you real?" I cried out in desperation. "Because if you aren't real, then truly I've lost everything. I've lost Shawn, who was my everything. But if I've lost you as well, then what do I have? Then I know I have nothing in this world."

In that moment of my brokenness, peace drifted over me. I sensed God's voice in my soul, reassuring, *I am real. I am alive. I am here.* I wept in God's presence, knowing that he had met me in this desolation.

In that darkest hour, I believe, beyond instinct or natural intuition, God was guiding me, assuring me. In the days and months ahead, he would lead my reasoning and show me that healing would be an ongoing process—a lifelong journey. I would need to dissect every part of grief I met along the way. More, I would need to meet the darkness that traversed my life on a warm September evening, experience it fully and own every piece of it, if I ever expected to know the other side.

Even in those rawest hours following Shawn's death, one thing became clear: I was convicted by a power beyond myself to be present and purposeful in every step of my grief journey. If I was ever to find life again, I would need to honor every part of the love my life had experienced.

I came to understand that I had been given something to share, and I trusted God would use my story. So I continued moving. It wasn't a movement I commanded. Rather, it was a series of choices to keep going, a progression lifting me in quiet conviction that I was where I was supposed to be.

Live now, it murmured.

How? my spirit whispered back.

I didn't hear a response.

"I don't know how," my heart cried, as I said the words out loud. "I can't believe this happened. I can't believe."

Then I heard. Solid. Even though I could not fully comprehend.

A pulse inside me, repeating one word—*Believe.*

Chapter 2

In the Line of Duty

i carry your heart (i carry it in my heart)

—E. E. CUMMINGS

Shawn and I played many secret games. Only he and I knew the rules.

One of the games was Questions. At random times during our marriage I'd ask Shawn, "Where is your heart?"

Without hesitation and on cue, he would place his hand over my heart and say, "Right here, Jen. You hold my heart. You know that."

Yes, I did. Still, I liked hearing him say it.

Then that awful day came, with the dark figures at my door. And he was gone. He took my heart with him.

The St. Paul *Pioneer Press* read, "Silvera, 32, was run down and killed Sept. 6 by a fugitive from South Dakota after placing stop sticks on I-35W in an effort to stop the man, who was driving a stolen vehicle and being pursued by police." Days later the newspaper announced, "The suspect, Steven Stanke, 26, has been charged in Anoka County District Court with three felonies, including second-degree murder."

The driver wasn't much younger than Shawn. Many young lives changed that day, causing me to think about age and life's unpredictability. Shortly after we were married I said to Shawn, "We should have married younger. Why did we wait until we were twenty-seven?"

"Because it was meant to be this way. We're more ready now to be married than we were then," he said, "then" referring to our high school days.

"But 'then' we would've had more years together," I said.

"We do have lots of years together," he replied. "Think about that. Think about all the time we still have together."

I thought ahead. Our plan included time—lots of time together for the two of us.

His death was defined by the police as "in the line of duty." Duty? Was this really what Shawn had committed himself to? Was this what I had devoted my heart to as his wife? This was not our plan. How can anyone commit to a plan that isn't their own?

According to the plan that I knew, people weren't supposed to die young and people weren't supposed to die at work. Yes, Shawn was a police officer, a risky profession, and I knew that he *could* die on duty, but I never imagined it would actually happen.

Shawn worked in law enforcement for over sixteen years and it was a good job fit. He once told me, "I can't believe I get paid for doing something I like so much."

Still, he didn't define his life around being a police officer. Only weeks before he was killed, he told me, "Jen, the best part of my day is when I come home to you, Jordan, and Madelynn." Shawn was most significantly my husband. He was my best friend and secret-keeper. My children's father. My partner, my confidant. My world.

Shawn didn't usually talk about his job unless asked. He'd discovered that some people have strong opinions about cops, sometimes based on experience, but most often supported by stereotypes that portray all police officers as inflexible, rigid, or arrogant.

But in Shawn I saw a police officer with a quiet diligence. It enabled him to remain confident in spite of judgment from others and gave him a steady dedication to do the right thing even when it might not be popular. For Shawn, police work was more than a job—it was a calling.

The truth is, police officers have a variety of personalities and interests that can't be typecast. And almost all of them have everyday lives with families, bills, home repairs, and the occasional vacation. Shawn was one of those everyday officers. He was the sandy, blond-haired, blue-eyed wonder I met in high school World Geography class, and who grew up to be a cop. I always thought of him as the cute boy I fell in love with when we were seventeen. The same boy who joined choir his senior year because he thought it made him well-rounded along with football practices and serving as vice president of student council.

For our fourth anniversary, Shawn surprised me with tickets to see the Broadway musical "The Pirates of Penzance" and reservations for an overnight stay at the Hilton. After the show, we lounged on the king-size bed, chins propped on folded arms with our feet on the white, down-feathered pillows as Shawn surfed cable channels.

He stopped surfing at a movie about two police partners. For fifteen minutes we watched a show about some tough-guy police officer—who made pottery in a back room of his house during his time off. Shawn laughed one of his deep belly whoops.

"This is so true," he told me, turning off the television and sitting up. "I knew this investigator who had insomnia because of job-related stress, and when he couldn't sleep he stayed up and did cross-stitch."

"Well, look at yourself," I said. "You love to cook, you sewed curtains for us when we lived in Honduras, you play the guitar, and you knew more about laundry than I did when we first got married. I bet you could even make some nice pottery if you tried."

"That's what I'm saying," he said. "People think cops are hard, tough. And maybe we are on the outside—it comes with the job. But you'd be surprised at all the hidden talents."

Now, all of Shawn's talents were gone. He had a full and loving life to share. None of our plans ever included this plot.

The evening the police officers came with the terrible news, they asked if I wanted to visit the site of the accident. Yes, I wanted to go.

We waited for family members to receive the news and come to my house. My parents were the first to arrive. Then everyone else seemed to get there at the same time. Shawn's mom, brother, and sister. My brother and three sisters. Once gathered, we were escorted by several squad cars to the ambulance. I rode in silence with Sergeant Bill. He didn't say much either, but did offer some explanation to prepare me for the scene. I tried to listen, but my thoughts kept returning to Shawn. I couldn't absorb the concept that he was dead. I wasn't sure that even seeing him would convince me. The heart has a hard time believing what it doesn't want to.

When we arrived, it was growing dark, and the night had a grotesque sense of festivity from the flashing lights of all the rescue vehicles. Over thirty officers, firefighters, and medics lined the road, standing at attention. As Sergeant Bill came around to open my door, a voice commanded, "Present arms." Suddenly in unison the entire line saluted. Walking along that line, I felt shielded by their presence as the salute remained in the position of honor. The ambulance, too, was shielded, draped by a tarp to veil it from swooping media helicopters.

A woman with kind eyes stepped forward. She touched my hand and introduced herself. Her eyes penetrated my spirit, telling me she cared and shared deep concern. I didn't catch her name, but she said, "Jennifer, I'll speak to you again soon." I nodded even though I didn't know what she meant. *Who was she? What would she tell me later?*

The line of officers held the salute until I entered the ambulance. "Order arms," the voice commanded. I stepped up and crawled into the back of the ambulance where I could see the tough, broken body strapped to a stretcher. Inside, an officer sat at Shawn's side, wiping his bleeding forehead. He quietly moved aside for me. A paramedic held Shawn's head, dutifully attending to him even though he was no longer there. She offered me consolation with her expression, but said nothing.

Here, surreal met real. On the stretcher was a man dressed in a police uniform. How could a police officer be the one hurt, bleeding, and killed, lying inside the ambulance? Why were all these people soothing him when he was employed to comfort others? He was the one trained to rescue, and now no one could rescue him.

Odd details. I first noticed the pen. Shawn always carried a pen in his shirt pocket. Even when he wasn't working. He'd tell me, "You never know when you'll need a pen." And we always laughed at how often someone would ask to borrow it. How did the pen stay in his pocket?

His body had been thrown nearly three hundred feet, the distance of a football field. Why did the pen survive, but not Shawn? Curse the stupid pen. It should have been ruined as well.

I examined as many details as I could, seeking evidence that would prove to my heart that he was actually never coming back. His navy blue short-sleeve uniform shirt was torn in a couple of places, but fewer than I expected. As if I would know what to expect. His shirt was repairable. We could wash it and mend it. Why couldn't he have survived like the shirt? Shouldn't he have survived?

His black, steeled-toed boot was crooked. I didn't point it out to anyone. But a foot isn't made to bend that way. Blood soaked his pant leg. The pants, though, weren't torn. This was deceiving. What appeared unharmed on the surface was damaged and disfigured underneath.

He'd left for work that afternoon looking healthy, clean-shaven, his hair still wet. His eyes were alive with intent. "Goodbye," he told me with a kiss, "I'll see you tonight. You'll wait up?"

He was a man full of life—loved fully by a family who defined their lives with him in it. Now his eyes were closed. Peaceful and lifeless. Why do those words go together? He couldn't look at me. He couldn't explain his side of the story. He couldn't offer me what he knew or felt or feared.

This couldn't be Shawn's story! *Shawn, look at me!* This is not how a love story is supposed to end. *Open your eyes.* If you could just see me, you wouldn't allow this to be happening.

His neck was swollen with clotted blood, a result of internal injuries caused by whiplash. The felon had decided to use the stolen car as a lethal weapon. Steering the three-thousand-pound piece of metal and traveling in excess of 110 miles per hour, Stanke purposefully aimed the car at Shawn. Shawn was hit on the right hamstring, instantaneously breaking his neck as his body ricocheted off the windshield. A year later at the trial, the accident reconstructionist would testify that Shawn had only six-tenths of a second to get out of the way.

On Shawn's face, slight black-and-blue marks had begun to form. War wounds. Death wounds. *This is not my Shawn.*

That's when a final detail came to me—his scent, strong and sweet. Then I knew it was him. This was my Shawn. His arm was warm. It looked unharmed, mildly tanned by the late summer sun. I couldn't help but touch it. I wanted to kiss him. I was afraid to. *Can I kiss death? Would it be inappropriate?* I kissed my fingers instead and touched them to his mouth.

Suddenly, my entire body felt the connection. His presence surrounded me, as if he were there. With everything around me so unfamiliar, I felt strangely like I was home—like he was home. For the first time since the horrific news, I could swallow and breathe and feel.

For the moment, I was myself. I didn't have to think about the mechanics of moving, and I could focus completely on him. This was my place—to be his helpmate. I was comfortable here. Maybe I could find a way to him, find a way to breathe life back into his lifeless body.

Irrational. Heartache doesn't look for logic in the midst of hurt.

"Jennifer, we're going to let some others take turns coming inside the ambulance." I didn't recognize the voice.

I was upset to be shaken out of my spell. The bond I had just experienced—warm inside of me—was fading to cold. Was I the one who had died? I wished for death to take me. *Let me die.* I wanted desperately to be wherever Shawn had gone. *Let me find a way to him.* Unreasonable. I kept my thoughts to myself.

Shawn's mom, siblings, my parents, other family members, and two of our closest childhood friends stood tense, waiting to enter. I didn't exchange glances with any of them, but I could feel them trembling. We were all shaken. While people rotated in and out of the ambulance, I remained by my husband's side, wishing against reason that I could invent a new secret game, wrap his raw, torn skin in bandages, create healing. *Shawn, I want to make this better. I'm so sorry you had to endure this trauma.* How could I make it go away?

After a brief time, which was actually about forty-five minutes, the woman with the kind eyes motioned for me to leave. "We need to transport his body to the hospital for an autopsy." She would take care of him.

Please let me stay here with him forever, I silently implored. I would bandage his broken legs, smooth the clotted veins, find a way to make his heart beat again. I would speak love to him, and he would heal, and then this nightmare could disappear. Isn't love stronger than death?

God, fix this! Make him well! I panicked. *If I can't do anything, you can!*
Disheartened, I rose. Nothing could change the circumstances.

I was ushered out of the ambulance. I never heard the command,
but the line of officers stood at attention again, saluting. I wasn't ready to
leave. I hadn't been given enough time! Why did I have to go? I felt like my
loyalty was being compromised, like I was betraying Shawn. My entire life
was in this vehicle. If I walked away, wasn't I leaving life behind?

Shawn owned my heart. My heart was in his heart.

How could I abandon my own heart?

Riding back home in the deepening darkness, I tried to imagine
Shawn's last moments. What were his last steps? His last words? His last
thoughts?

His partner would later tell me that Shawn took three, gaping strides.
The coroner, the lady with the kind eyes, Dr. Amatouzio, corroborated
this fact at the trial. Her evidence on the position of injuries affirmed
that Shawn had, indeed, been running for his life. In court she testified,
"Shawn was running with full force from sunset to sunrise." In his last
moments, he'd fought to escape, fought to come home to us.

In my mind I see him, as in a vision, poised to throw the stop sticks.
He will have a grand story to reenact when he gets home. Then everything changes. The driver of the car swerves, aiming to hit him, giving
Shawn less time than can be counted to react. In the charcoal-black
backdrop of the night, I hear one word, one scream, clear and sharp.

Jennifer!

No one heard Shawn shout. No one was near enough. Still I sense his
last thought was of me and our children. I believe Shawn's every wish for
our happiness and prayer for our comfort was on his last breath. I envision
an instant where life stood motionless. I hear my name. Only God knows.

There were two command centers. The police department was in full
action, responding to an officer's death. All the Lino Lakes officers were
immediately taken off their shifts, which were covered through the generosity of the surrounding Anoka Hennepin County agencies. For a week

the department's new focus was to plan and organize an honorable burial for their fallen officer. The family's goal was the same. My home became the second command center where, over the next five days, details were made for the wake and funeral.

The media response was tremendous. A list of newspapers and news stations wanted quotes. Shawn's brother, Mark, helped respond to some of the many calls. Sergeant Bill had practically taken up residence at my home, and with each passing hour, he had new information about who would be attending the very public funeral.

The second day into planning, he knocked on my bedroom door. "Jennifer, Governor Pawlenty is on the phone for you."

I hesitated as I took the phone, pen in hand. Writing had become a way for me to calm my swirling thoughts.

"Jennifer," said the governor, "I'm on my way to Newark and apologize for the background noise in the airport, but wanted to call before I have to board. I was just given the tragic news of your husband."

"Thank you, sir, for calling," I said.

"I want to offer you the deepest condolences from myself and on behalf of the entire state of Minnesota. Your husband is a hero. His life was taken entirely too early. But, please know we recognize him as a symbol of someone who lived a strong life of purpose."

My heart was warmed. "Shawn admired you, sir. He believed in your work and supported your leadership."

There was a noticeable pause. "I'm humbled, Jennifer, especially at a time when we should all be comforting you. I'm touched, and I guess I'll only be able to thank your husband tonight with my prayers. I will offer my gratitude for his sacrifice."

I thanked the governor for calling and handed Sergeant Bill his cell phone.

Sergeant Bill hung up the phone and said, "You make me nervous with your writing everything down."

"I don't want to forget anything," I told him. "Someday my kids will have many questions for me and I'll want to tell them everything."

Sergeant Bill only smiled. Then lowering his head he added, "We'll always be here for you and the kids—for what it's worth."

There were many other things I'd want to tell my children someday. For instance, that the governor ordered all U.S. and Minnesota flags to be flown at half-staff on capitol grounds and throughout the state from sunrise until sunset on the twelfth of September in honor and remembrance of Officer Shawn B. Silvera.

As had become our new custom, Sergeant Bill was our escort the morning of the funeral. As he buckled my kids in the back seat, he had more updates.

"The governor has agreed to speak at your request. He didn't want to use Shawn's funeral as a platform. Still, you need to know he's honored that you asked him. That is the precise message I was to give you. He was completely honored."

I sat calmly, waiting to see if there was more.

"There'll be other dignitaries present . . . other state representatives and officials. Bishop Pates has left his retreat early, and he'll be attending as well."

It was evident that Sergeant Bill was glad to have something positive to report after so much sadness.

"I'll be speaking too," I told him.

"Oh . . . Was that in the program?"

"No. I'm not sure if I can do it. But I'm going to try."

"That will be strong, Jennifer." He paused. "When did this transpire?"

"This morning," I replied. "I wrote out my thoughts before you got here. It seems to help when I write."

After the private and final viewing of Shawn at the funeral home, his family joined our vehicle and we processed to the church. Three other Suburbans followed ours, carrying immediate and extended family members. Next in line were all the Lino Lakes police squads, the Centennial Fire cars, and one squad from each Anoka Hennepin agency. Many troopers and motorcyclists trailed the procession in the pouring rain.

An officer who dies in the line of duty is given a full honors funeral—a military funeral. Shawn's was modeled after President Kennedy's. As our procession crept through the streets, people lined the sidewalks, waving to pay respect. A sea of children stood on an elementary football field, drenched in the rain, as the hearse and our line of cars passed. They held their hands over their hearts and recited the pledge of allegiance. Nothing has ever touched my heart with such a mark of respect and pride. Shawn was an everyday hero.

When I got out of the car, hundreds of officers stood at attention, line upon line of them. They stood completely still, saluting, as if they didn't notice the rain trickling down their faces, down their starched uniforms. If honor could be touched, this is what it would feel like.

The service was a tribute to a life well lived. My complete sorrow was mixed with a sense of joy in sharing Shawn's love with others. It comforted me to know that my husband had influenced many lives in a powerful way. Our priest, Father Reiser, spoke about Shawn's legacy, about Shawn's life being fulfilled in his answering of God's call, and that Shawn died doing his duty. With this message in mind, Father Reiser encouraged each member of the audience to do their duty daily—meet the challenges of each day and live out their own life's mission.

The governor was the first to give a eulogy, sharing the symbolism of the thin blue line. A thin line of police officers helps to prevent civilized society from descending into chaos. It also refers to the brotherhood of the profession, a bond between officers, which is taken very seriously. He spoke, too, of his admiration for Shawn, for his life lived with integrity, passion, and ultimately heroism.

Shawn's brother spoke after the governor and talked about Shawn's fun-loving personality and how growing up they were best friends. I knew that Shawn had looked up to Mark in many ways, and now Mark professed that he had done the same.

The chief of police, our priest, and two long-time friends followed. Each shared their grief at Shawn's untimely death, and their admiration for Shawn's love of life.

His lifelong, childhood friend, Scott, added a lighter moment. One summer, after they'd both been working in law enforcement for a few years, Shawn joined Scott for a ride-along. As they were driving that night, Shawn confessed, "You know, Scott, when I'm on patrol, helping to keep everything safe and in order, I feel like Batman!"

Occasionally, Shawn would share memorable incidents connected with his work, and he was an animated storyteller—acting out parts, making faces, imitating voices. It is the context in which he told them, though, that is most clear—around a table of close-knit family or friends, the handful of people whom he felt comfortable with. This was my husband, who loved to share his life.

Now I was sharing him with over three thousand people, whose attendance marked one of the largest and longest law enforcement funerals in the history of Minnesota. People later mentioned that the mass lasted nearly four hours. I could have stayed there all day, surrounded by people whom Shawn's life had touched and listening to story after story about him—some of which I was hearing for the first time.

The wake the night before was attended by an equal number, if not more, inside the church's gymnasium. The line to greet our family wrapped around the hallways into the parking lot, in spite of the hot, muggy night. My college friends Andrea, Cindy, and Megan stayed by my side as I nodded in numb response, receiving the embrace of a hurting community. The honor guard stood post, sweat dripping from their brows, never moving, out of respect for a fallen officer.

I would be the last to speak. My eulogy was a final proclamation of love to Shawn. From the podium I looked beyond the sea of faces and into the memories connected to this church building. I knew this place like my own home. Growing up, I had been confirmed in this church. I was a bride in this church, Shawn and I played music in the band at church and helped with the youth group. I'd played the mahogany grand piano tucked in the choir section many times. This church was like a friend to me.

Now this church would hold another, unspeakably sad, memory—the place where I buried my best friend. Standing in the place I connected to my faith I wondered, *what do I believe now?*

CHAPTER 3

Our Love Story

Is it possible to carry magic in a voice?
I hear you say my name and remind myself to breathe.
I see your eyes smile and I am taken in . . .
I hold my breath until life comes back again.

—JENNIFER, TO SHAWN
January 4, 1999

From the podium at church, our story played out in my mind like a slide show. And watching it, though I don't believe in fairy tales, I can see how they are born. Ours began in high school.

My junior year I was learning about more than just memorizing North American mountain ranges. I was discovering this boy named Shawn Silvera. I taught piano lessons to his little sister, Nikki, which led Shawn and me to our first conversation.

"Nikki's been playing her song for the piano recital ten times a day," Shawn told me, turning his desk sideways to make it easier to talk.

"That's impressive," I said. I'd been quizzing Nikki for months during her lessons to find out more about her brother.

"Shawn, turn your desk around," said Mr. Biggins. "We're not working in groups today."

I giggled at this friendly boy making a show of turning his desk forward. I envied his self-assurance, so different from my shyness. And I liked his ocean-blue eyes. Unique, mystical.

"Are you trying out for the talent show?" Shawn asked, turning his head toward me.

"Yes," I said, my voice low, hoping Mr. Biggins wouldn't catch us talking again. I wasn't as brave as this boy.

Shawn leaned closer. "I'm going to play a song on the piano."

"You know how to play piano?" I asked. Nikki had never told me that.

"Not really. But I taught myself some stuff," he said, as if it were the same as tying a shoe. "What I'd really love to learn is guitar."

"That'd be cool," I said, looking down at my books, pretending to read.

"Are you going to the game tonight?" he asked. Shawn played running back for the football team.

"Yeah. Jami, Shelly, and I will be there," I said. We always went to the games on Friday night and then to Pizza Hut for garlic-cheesy bread and Dr. Pepper.

"Maybe I'll see you," he said and turned around. Mr. Biggins was staring at us.

Shawn and I hung out a few times that summer and started dating the first of September our senior year. He took me to a quaint restaurant called the Signature Café in a charming residential area of southeast Minneapolis. It was a husband-and-wife operation, serving authentic Egyptian food. We ordered their freshly made babaganoosh served with warm pita bread and sandwiches.

When it was time to pay, Shawn looked at the bill then looked startled as he grabbed for his wallet.

"Hey, do you have any money?" he asked.

I thought he was teasing, but his expression told me he wasn't. I handed him a five-dollar bill, which didn't leave much for a tip. Shawn ran out to his dad's truck and scrounged for orphaned quarters under the seat. He came back inside with another dollar, laid it on the table, and we snuck out.

I was a little embarrassed and a little bothered. How could this guy ask me on a date and not bring enough money? If Shawn was at all embarrassed, though, it didn't show. He didn't belabor the blunder—just apologized as we drove to the state capitol to walk around the grounds.

His confidence intrigued me, and soon we were both chuckling over the incident. Who was this guy who was so sure of himself? When he brought me home that night, we sat in the truck for a moment in front of my parents' house. He told me that his mom had said, "People should never kiss on the first date." I could tell he respected her. I could also tell he was toying with this rule about first dates. He leaned closer to me. I tried to sit still, keeping both hands under my legs, but I felt as jittery as a firefly. I hoped he wouldn't notice.

"You act as if you've never been kissed before," Shawn told me.

I didn't say anything, but raised my eyebrows.

"You haven't been kissed before?" Shawn asked.

"Nope," I found one word.

"Well, it's easy. You don't have to worry," he said.

I think Shawn was pleased with the idea of teaching me. Just as he put his arm on the back of the seat behind my shoulders, the front-porch light flickered on and off about four times. We both jumped as if we'd been caught skinny dipping.

"Oh gosh . . . well . . ." I fumbled for words. "I guess I'd better go."

I snatched my white sweater, the one it had taken me over an hour to decide on bringing, which I ended up not even using. Mortified, I raced to the house. I was sure Shawn would never try to kiss me again. He might not even ask me on another date!

If I could see the smile in your eyes, I would feel like
I was seventeen again, meeting you for the first time.
Then we could start our journey all over.

One week later Shawn did take me on another date and succeeded in being my first kiss. That would be the first of many good things he brought to my life.

Dating at a young age, we were cautious about saying, "I love you." We were idealistic. We agreed that love is more than a feeling. Love means waiting for that special person. Love means long commitment. It was a word intended to be long-lasting. Can one really make a lasting decision at the age of seventeen?

Still, we knew that something was happening between us, and we wanted to invent our own secret expression. We couldn't say, "I like you." That sounded like something you tell your camp counselor. One day on a whim, Shawn signed a note to me, "I 'something' you." That started a phrase we'd use on many occasions.

We dated our entire senior year. The summer after graduation we talked about "us." I was infatuated with Shawn, but I also wanted to explore, uncover new ideas and travel to different places. I'd enrolled at St. Olaf College in Northfield, Minnesota, to study psychology and sociology. Shawn had different college plans, so we agreed to "just be friends."

Shawn stayed in our hometown of Coon Rapids, Minnesota, focused and serious about earning a law enforcement degree. Putting himself through school, he worked full-time for the Coon Rapids Police Department as a Community Service Officer—that's the person who gets all the calls involving stray cats and sweet old ladies who hear noises at night.

We couldn't fully explain why it wasn't yet the time for "us," but it was hard for my heart to stay away from him. During my winter break freshman year, we saw each other, talked a lot. On the last night of break, we sat across from one another in a booth at a fast-food restaurant.

At the time, a strong believer in destiny, I told Shawn, "We can't be 'just friends.' That doesn't work for me. It has to be all or nothing."

He looked at me as if I were presenting an unsolvable riddle.

I continued, "If it's meant to be, love will come back. Even if it's five years from now you can't keep love apart."

"Then it's nothing," he said.

Once the words were said aloud I realized they weren't what I wanted to hear. Not until years later did I discover the intricacies of communication between men and women. Often when one *says* something, the other *hears* something different. It turns out that Shawn had wanted to stay together all along but didn't want to inhibit my desire to explore. With part pride, part sacrifice, he freed me to discover myself.

Later that night, one of the girls from my dorm, Melissa, picked me up and we drove back to campus. I cried the entire way. I had never been so conflicted. I wanted to have a big adventure, but I also wanted Shawn to say, "I want everything with you." I'd hoped we could have the adventure together.

During our college years Shawn and I remained indecisive about our relationship. I spent time studying in Guatemala, Ecuador, and Colombia and after graduation traveled with a music group, Celebrant Singers, throughout the United States, Iceland, and more of Latin America. I became fascinated by other cultures, and especially with the Spanish language. I wanted to become fluent.

Every time I came home for a break, though, I wondered what Shawn was doing. Still, when we'd call each other or unexpectedly run into each other, neither of us knew how to express exactly what we wanted. I blamed most of this hesitancy on my unsettled spirit. I seemed to be searching the world over for what was right in front of me.

One night on the phone, Shawn said to me, "You're waiting for life to be perfect, Jennifer. Life doesn't work that way."

When he'd bring me home after an evening together and I didn't want it to end, I'd tease, "Let's run away to Canada."

He'd play along for a while. "When?"

"Right now," I'd say.

"We can't do that. I have a job. You have school."

"Let's just go anyway," I'd say. "Then we'll be together. No distractions."

His reply was always, "I wish we could."

Often the deep thinker, these were times that I allowed myself to be whimsical. Maybe to balance me, he remained rational. I didn't want him to be logical though. Still, I wondered what I'd *really* do if one day he called my bluff and just started driving north.

There was a sort of catch-22 between us. Shawn wanted my complete, unconditional love—for me to give up my world in exchange for loving him. Could I dedicate myself entirely? I wanted Shawn to take a chance on me—to risk everything for the sake of love. I wanted him to tell me honestly how he felt instead of what he *thought* I wanted to hear. This could be dangerous, because he could be rejected.

Someone had to choose to stop running—first.

Three years after I graduated with my bachelor's degree in family studies, Shawn cornered me in the church parking lot. We'd come out of a music rehearsal for the worship team—I played piano and he now played guitar.

"We're meant to be together," he told me.

"How do you know?" I asked, no longer so whimsical, once again calculating everything in my life.

"Because we're better people together than we are apart," he said.

When I got to my car, I found a torn piece of scratch paper. On it were written three little words: "I 'Something' You."

Years later, Shawn told me the other part of the conversation that night, which he never spoke out loud. He promised himself, "I'll pursue her until she's convinced. If we don't end up together, it won't be because of me."

Less than a year later, on a warm breezy night on the first of September, Shawn surprised me. He'd created an open-air restaurant with white linens, candles, and his mom's china underneath the Witch's Hat water tower overlooking the skyline of Minneapolis. His sister Nicole guarded the setting until we arrived. She videotaped our entrance and then disappeared.

The music from the Disney movie *Aladdin* played on a small boom box underneath the card table. In his pocket, Shawn carried a ring, which his brother Mark had helped him pick out. On my place setting lay a single red rose and a handmade card declaring his love for me. This was more than "something." Then he proposed.

He was taking a chance. He was loving in all measure, telling me exactly how he felt. I was stunned . . . and, typical for me, I was processing.

"Shawn, we haven't talked about this," I told him.

"We're talking now," he said. He was nervous and calm at the same time.

"We don't even know how we want to raise kids, balance finances, or handle disagreements," I said.

I don't know where this checklist came from.

"We'll read a book," he said.

"What about living abroad? I still want to learn Spanish, and I can't do that by staying in Minnesota."

"I'll go with you," he said.

"You'll go with me?" I asked—both eyebrows raised in disbelief.

"Yes. If you want to fly to some third-world country and eat beans and rice for a couple of years, I'll go with you. If you want to go to Canada, I'm there. If you change your mind and pick an entirely new location, that's okay with me."

His entire expression told me it was okay to stop considering all the outcomes.

"I want to be with you, Jen," he vowed. "It doesn't matter to me where we go, where we live, where we work, what we eat . . . I want to do this thing called life with you."

There it was. He'd done it. He'd risked everything for the sake of loving me in all measure.

"Ask me again," I said.

"What?" he said confused.

"You know. Ask me again. The whole 'Will you marry me' thing."

Getting down on one knee, he took both of my hands in his. "Jennifer, will you be my wife? I want you by my side. I want to be by yours. Will you marry me?"

I surrendered. Without having all the answers. No more waiting for every piece of life to be perfect.

"It would be my complete honor."

Shawn and I were married on May 12, 2000. I was thrilled to be his wife. He was right; we were better people together than apart. I knew we were made for each other, and I relished the time we spent together.

When, as the director of human resources for a major hotel chain, I traveled several times for training seminars, Shawn went with me. I helped him with his D.A.R.E. (Drug Abuse Resistance Education) projects that he taught at the elementary school. We were involved with music ministry at church, and we spent any free time hanging out, creating fun dinners for friends and family, or reading books in bed.

We were also tested during our first year of marriage. My perfectionism caused many arguments. I was particular and wanted things done in a certain way. The week before we were married my bridesmaid, Jami, was helping me move some things into our new apartment. Shawn was in the kitchen unpacking boxes. I noticed a loaf of bread on the counter and immediately became irritated.

Grabbing the bread to throw it in the refrigerator I asked my future spouse, "How can you leave bread on the counter like this? It will go bad."

Puzzled, Shawn looked at me and said, "Growing up my mom always kept bread by the toaster and—"

I didn't let him finish. "Well, my mom taught us girls to keep bread in the refrigerator. She keeps everything in the refrigerator. That way it stays fresh longer."

With indifference, Shawn went back to the task of unpacking. I, however, couldn't get past my newfound issue of where to store bread.

"Shawn, what are we going to do about this?" I asked.

Jami stood quietly by the kitchen table during the awkward interaction. Out of loyalty to me she didn't comment, although her eyes seemed to say, *poor Shawn*. She later told me I was just having a pre-wedding meltdown.

My meticulousness was often a strength, but it could also be a strong weakness. Shawn worked hard to please me and still I would find the one thing left undone instead of appreciating all the ways he was working to help me. Growing in our marriage, I started to discover I couldn't continually make an excuse for my behavior. Life isn't perfect. People aren't perfect. Grace needs to accompany relationships.

Shawn was stubborn. If we disagreed on something he would pout and ignore the confrontation rather than actually discuss the situation with me. I couldn't comprehend this lack of communication. I wanted to discuss things in minute detail.

On one occasion, we performed a defiant sort of dance around each other for over three days, barely exchanging glances let alone words. The more I approached my husband to work things out, the less he responded.

On the fourth day, after neither of us could tolerate much more silence, Shawn came to me and said, "I know we need to talk. I don't want to live like this." It took much practice and humility, but he worked hard in our marriage to change old habits by trying again. Communication is vital for a healthy relationship and it rarely comes without effort.

Where is the balance in relationships? We were often overwhelmed with how to love each other. Where were the feelings that were supposed to accompany love? We held strong to our belief that love is more than a feeling. What we were learning was even more profound—love is work. Love is very hard work. It takes constant attention and practice. But it is the most worthwhile kind of work.

Shawn liked to wrap Christmas presents layered in several boxes. Each had to be opened, one layer at a time, to find what was in the last, tiniest box. Our love was like that. As we slowly unfolded different truths about ourselves and our relationship in areas of pride, communication, forgiveness, and acceptance, each layer of truth we unwrapped brought us closer to the gift of loving better.

We uncovered the paradox of serving. We called it our "cup of water in the middle of the night"—something we'd read in our favorite book, *A Severe Mercy*. A husband and wife practiced doing small acts of kindness and service selflessly for the other. If one spouse asked for something, the other would willingly help if he or she could. The cup-of-water-in-the-middle-of-the-night stood for the imagery. What else could be more gracious and selfless than getting out of a warm bed to get something to drink for someone else? When I stopped thinking primarily about myself, I found more peace as I adapted to married life. And the more I served Shawn, the more he served my life.

Of course, this practice isn't to be misused. Then it becomes manipulation rather than service out of love. Being coerced to serve causes resentment. Choosing to serve reinforces a relationship.

When I was pregnant, I was sometimes uncomfortable at night; right about the time Shawn was getting off work and crawling into bed. Lying next to me, he'd often ask what he could do for me, and I would literally request a drink of water. Every time he got out of bed to bring me something to drink, I thought, *this guy loves me.*

The longer we were together, the word *love* didn't seem to fully encompass our experience. We decided that the English language needed more words in its vocabulary to describe love. The Greeks have multiple ways to express love: love for friendship, love that is passionate, love for objects, love for God, and love that is unconditional. How can one word be adequate to express all the ways to love? I love my dog. I love my job. I love my cup of coffee. I love our new carpet. I love our kids. I love springtime. I love getting my hair cut. I love you.

Later in our life together, we brought back our secret phrase: *I "something" you.* Like watercolors on canvas, our invented expression represented the different shades of love; it pictured where we had been and where we were going.

We were going somewhere together.

We had a quirky, fun holiday just for the two of us: our *month-a-versary.* We originally designed the dates at the suggestion of Father Reiser, the priest who'd married us. He encouraged us to honor and recognize our marriage each month rather than wait to celebrate once a year—to set aside time to share what we valued and to work on ways to strengthen our relationship.

Shawn brought me flowers on the twelfth of every month. Most often he brought white daisies because they'd last almost to the next month. I'd make a special dinner, breakfast, or snack, depending on what our schedules allowed. Some months we swapped—I'd bring a gift and Shawn would cook. One time he delved into making lobster.

Our simplest celebrations, though, were shared while we were stationed in Central America with the Peace Corps. After a year of marriage, we'd decided to explore a mission of service as a way to share our talents and experience an adventure together—just as Shawn had promised when he proposed.

After being accepted to work with small-business development projects, we were stationed in a tiny, poverty-stricken village in southern Honduras. This was a significant time for us, building a strong foundation in the early stage of our marriage. Far away from family, the distractions of jobs and friends, and other pressures that could potentially hinder our relationship, we learned to truly rely on one another.

With no indoor plumbing and limited electricity, we boiled our drinking water and took cold bucket-baths. Food had to be kept in airtight containers, safe from insects and rodents. Sleeping with scorpions was an adjustment, and we referred to the iguana that lived in our clay ceiling tiles as our "nosy neighbor."

We savored care packages sent from home. One day a package arrived from Mark.

"Look, Jen! Beef jerky," Shawn said as he started to tear open the bag.

"Don't open it!" I told him.

"Why not?" he asked. "This whole box is loaded with other treats—cappuccino mixes, granola bars, chocolate."

"Let's wait to enjoy it. We should save the beef jerky for a time we're really desperate," I told him.

"Like now?" he replied.

"No, like later," I said.

"I've already waited four weeks for this padded envelope to get here," he teased.

"But, you didn't even know you were waiting for it!" I said, loving a good debate.

Shawn knew that I also loved anticipation—nearly as much as I loved gifts. He rolled his eyes at me and threw the jerky into the plastic bin where we stored our food. That night, reading late, Shawn convinced me it was "later," and we enjoyed beef jerky at midnight.

These were uncomplicated days. We learned to live with only the essentials, appreciating any extras as blessings. Our fanciest food while living overseas was a box of macaroni and cheese, which Shawn's mom had sent. We saved it for our month-a-versary and valued it as much as any lobster.

We used to write letters to each other on our yearly wedding anniversaries. Signed and sealed, they remained unopened, never read by the other spouse. This practice of secret-letter writing started on our first anniversary when we drove up to the Canadian border, just so we could say we'd been to another country. I loved to drive with Shawn. He was a patient listener, and I enjoyed hours with just the two of us.

When we arrived in Canada we found a peninsula of rocks on a clear, pristine lake encircled by tall, lean pine trees. The early May day was calm, the water a sheer reflection, the air crisp. Ignoring the chill, we basked in the sun, which, if we really pretended, provided a minimal amount of warmth.

I suddenly remembered a notebook in the back seat of the car. I ran to grab it, wanting to record my impressions. That's when we got the idea to individually record the meaning and the high points of our first year of marriage through letters to each other.

We didn't have an exact plan for the letters. I suggested we read all of them on our twentieth wedding anniversary. Shawn's idea was to begin opening them, one a year, after twenty years of marriage, as a way to celebrate our next twenty years together. Either way, we had to wait— another gift of anticipation.

Pulling myself back to the present, I gazed down the carpeted aisle that I'd walked as a bride. Without noticing the crowd of people, I read to Shawn as if he and I were the only two people in the sanctuary.

September 12, 2005

Dearest Shawn,

What am I supposed to say to you today? What would sound most eloquent? What am I supposed to tell people about you? What would give you the most honor? How can I write about you when you were my favorite writer? And how can I tell about you when you were my favorite speaker? And how can I play music for you when you were my favorite musician? And how can I create a day of much beauty and celebration for you when you were my favorite artist?

I love you. And I would be lying if I said I don't miss you. For I miss you beyond what I can describe; I miss you with every part of my being.

I am blessed to have known you—not only as your wife but as your best friend. In you I found my soul's mate. If I could talk to you today, I would not waste a single breath on things that don't matter. I would tell you, "You are perfect for me even in the midst of our imperfections." If I could see you today, I would just love you. I would simply love you. I wouldn't waste one minute not loving you.

I see you everywhere. When I wake, you are my first thought. I see you in the quiet places of my mind, in the faces of Jordan and Maddi, in the details of our home. I see you, Shawn, everywhere.

I see you in the people who loved you when you were young. I see you in the tears of your mom. I see you in the heart of your sister. I see you in the fierce loyalty of your brother, and I see you in the grace of those who loved you.

I see you in the bravery of your work, in the passions of your life, in friendships tried and true, and in the honor of the men and women who daily fight the good fight to protect and serve.

I smell you in the T-shirt you wore to work on your last day. The scent of strength lingers in the air. The scent of your life surrounds me. I taste you in the air I breathe and only wish I could breathe it back into you.

I hear you in my thoughts speaking comfort to my mind, whispering truth to my fears, singing a love song to me. I see and feel and smell and taste and hear you everywhere. I see and feel and smell and taste and hear that God is still good.

Your love is life to me.

If I could sing to you, Shawn, I would sing with my best voice. And yet my song would be empty, until I could sing again with you. And if I could hold your hand, I would feel stronger. The truest love I know is to have loved you and to have been loved by you. The best gift you have given me through your sacrifice is that I have now seen the best in people, and it is beautiful.

The only way I can honor you is through the witness of my life. To meet people where they are at and to accept them for who they are and share the unconditional love you taught me. For I can now see how good people are, and your deep commitment to protect and help them.

I do not feel abandoned. I feel the prayers of thousands holding me up. Now I see all the gifts I had in you and all the gifts I continue to receive from you in the people you left behind to care for me. I never could have imagined you would send an army of angels to cover me with gifts.

I am sad, but not from the life I lived with you—for it was full and it was good. I am sad and I am broken for the life I will live without you. Your joy was my joy. Your pain was my pain. Your love was my love, and I am forever changed by you.

Shawn—you lived an authentic, purpose-driven life. You taught me not to hide. I am here with you now, Shawn. I love you.

After the funeral mass, the rain stopped as if planned, and a procession went on foot to the graveyard behind the church. My kids, who'd been in the nursery, joined me for the burial. My sister Cynthia carried Maddi, who kept looking at the sky. I held Jordan, who was pointing up at the clouds.

We walked behind the riderless horse, a tradition dating back to early military days when the horse without a rider followed the hearse. The stirrups carry empty boots, facing backward to symbolize that even in death, the fallen officer still leads. And they who come behind will aim to follow his leadership of bravery, courage, and valor.

The sun poked through the clouds, as if on cue, spilling vertical rays down to the earth. I felt it as a message to me that God's grace had touched the entire day.

Believe in me, said the message. *I am here.*

PART TWO

GRIEF

shattered, shaken
where is my strength?

given, taken
where is my faith?

reaching, longing
where is grace?

bring me back
to a steady place

broken spirit
be brave

JENNIFER'S NOTES
untitled, undated

CHAPTER 4

Gray

If you must tell me your opinions, tell me what you
believe in. I have plenty of doubts of my own.

—JOHANN GOETHE

With plenty of doubts swirling around, it's hard to believe in anything after loss. Shawn's death was never part of my plan for a perfect life, but a picture can quickly be altered. Before Shawn's death, I was naive and trusting. In an instant, everything changed.

In the months following the funeral I was plagued by uncertainty, mistrust, and doubt. At times I'd be suddenly overcome by the reality that Shawn was actually dead, that I'd never see him again on this earth. I questioned what I'd always believed in, and wondered if this gray place I'd entered would be my permanent residence.

My body continued operating, but without my total self present. It's as if my spirit recoiled from the horrible reality. Some might call this a state of denial, but it's something deeper. It's life in a holding pattern—the body appears to function while beneath the surface the spirit continues to grieve. This was my new state of normal, and I was frightened by this completely unknown territory.

My belief in the reality of my loss, of my perspectives, and of God became riddled with doubt. Forty-five days after Shawn died, I wrote in my journal,

I am at a loss of how to express myself. At moments
during the day I try to suppress how I feel in order
to continue with the tasks at hand. In order to
function in my role as a mom with young children,
I merely endure the slow passing of minutes.

I give myself pep talks throughout the day, trying to
convince myself that if I live without feeling too deeply,
I will be able to survive. I rationalize that if I am
able to get through a moment without extreme
sensation—neither high joy nor low sadness—and
can maintain that even level where all feelings are
dull or numb, then I will be able to carry on.

Life has taken on a new color: gray.
At present, I don't see in color. Nothing is bright
or exuberant. Nothing stands out. Nothing
engages me. I feel disconnected.

At odd moments I am stabbed all over again
that this is a real story, happening to real people, a real
mom, and a real baby boy and a real baby girl.
And how I respond to this story will make all the
difference in not only my life, but theirs as well. This is
a heavy responsibility. Especially on days that
I would rather cover up my head with my favorite
down comforter and ignore the day altogether.

Being a mom doesn't allow me this luxury. In the
famous words of my grandmother, "Life goes on." Today
those words offer little comfort. The words may be truthful,
but I am nowhere near facing the truth. I still have secret
wishes that Shawn will come home tonight.

It's possible to understand something without truly comprehending it. We can understand the concept of Christ and his sacrifice on the cross, for example, without comprehending it. When we reach comprehension we get the total significance of it and its implications for *our lives*.

This is the way I felt about Shawn's death. I understood that he'd died, but I hadn't yet comprehended it. One evening a few months after Shawn died, I went out to dinner with friends. Among their other inquiries, they asked me, "When did it really hit you?"

I couldn't answer. I wasn't sure how to respond, and for days I carried the question around in my mind. Events of tragic magnitude do not suddenly connect with the cognitive mind and we say, "Oh! Now I get it! I can keep going, now that this terrible thing has been explained. All things work for good—so the Bible says, so I'll just focus on the good."

No! The defiant contrary. I understood clearly what had happened. I was aware of the huge loss. But the full significance and implications of Shawn's death hadn't "hit" me. Rather, it trickled in. I couldn't, in fact, find a way to escape the gradual revealing of what his death meant.

Like timed-release capsules, reminders of his absence seeped into my system in small doses. Each morning was a new, rude waking. I opened my eyes, only to be weighed down by a heavy knowledge that life had changed dramatically, that someone very important was missing. Night after night, as I got into bed, I felt like I was being crushed in the realization that Shawn wouldn't, couldn't, come back.

In retrospect, I sense that if we absorb all the implications of our loss all at once, we might be pushed into complete devastation. The impact would be more than the body and soul is designed to endure.

Months after that dinner with friends, I wanted to explain to them, "It wasn't possible for me to be 'hit' by Shawn's death. I couldn't take a blow that big! Let me stagger through this new life for a bit and then get back to you. Maybe in a year or two I'll finally realize the full extent of what has happened."

On many mornings I awoke completely despondent. My journal entries were heavy, dark. Even though they brought some relief, with my lack of energy they were a burden to write.

One night I woke in absolute terror. "God," I cried out into the shadows, "What do you want from me?"

In distress, I found my journal and began writing.

> *Why are you bringing me through this passage of grief?*
> *It is too much for me. It was easier to follow you when my*
> *belief in your goodness had not yet been challenged.*
> *It was easier to hope when life was good.*

> *Now I am being tested, and I question everything*
> *I have ever been taught. I doubt my beliefs. I am*
> *struggling to trust in the faith that, before, I accepted*
> *without question. I am searching to find that you,*
> *God, are still faithful, even when the results of your*
> *faithfulness don't match my desires. Is it wrong*
> *to think, God, you made a mistake?*

> *Can you reach into my being? Can you reach*
> *down as far as the hurt? Can you fill each crevice that*
> *was gouged into me on the day Shawn died? Maybe I*
> *shouldn't ask what you want from me. Maybe I should*
> *pray and plead for what I need from you. I need you to*
> *be true. But I have no idea what the truth is anymore.*
> *Replace my doubts with your truth.*

I closed the journal and dragged myself back into bed—exhausted but somehow comforted. I didn't have answers, but at least I was looking for them.

My doubts were pushing me to search for more. I wanted to find meaning again for my life. But with my belief system shattered, where could I start?

I started with God. It was hard for me to admit that I had doubts about my faith—but God knew it anyway. So I opened myself up to him. Rather than forcing myself to pack away my disbelief, I asked God to help me with it. Just knowing that God was bigger than my uncertainty gave me something to hope for.

As the months passed, I continued to feel removed from life. Time did not heal the discord in my soul. Life as I had known it had ended, and now I waited for it to actually be over. I had no intention of suicide, but all desire to engage in life was gone. Confused, I prayed at night that God would take me in my sleep, while at the same time praying that my children would not lose another parent. Life had nothing to offer me, and I had nothing to give back to life.

My brother, Adam, called one night, as he frequently did, to check up on me.

"Do you feel like coming out with Lori and me this weekend?" he asked. "My band is playing on Friday night if you want to come listen."

"I'll see," I told him. *No*, I thought. I didn't want to do anything. I didn't want to go to movies or watch television or eat out or eat in. I only wanted what I'd lost—my husband.

"Well, maybe I can come up on Sunday to see the kids," he replied.

"They would love that." They would, I knew. My kids were so little that, in some ways, they were shielded from grief.

But for me, the dread of life without Shawn ran through my days. I appeared functional on the outside, able to take care of my toddlers, shop for groceries, even go out for dinner with friends. But inside I was collapsing as the life I preferred and desperately wanted back crumbled and disappeared.

Full of despair, I could not see hope. I tried to see a positive picture, but the jagged edge of my loss quickly tore it apart. The only thing I truly hoped for was that someone would knock on my door with the same urgency as on the day Shawn died, and inform me that I was getting my life back.

After a profound loss, daily tasks become new challenges, and it's difficult to complete one simple item on a to-do list. I'd always been goal oriented, but after Shawn's death I found it hard to trust my own abilities. I felt out of balance, struggling to concentrate or make sense of the world around me.

Nearly six months after Shawn died, I tried to use a coupon at the grocery store. The clerk was not unkind, but handed it back to me saying, "Ma'am, I'm sorry, but this expired last summer."

I was stunned, and felt that surely time had tricked me. I tried to act as if this was just a simple mistake, one that could easily have occurred when Shawn was alive, and not yet another of the landslides my life had become—the missed appointments, always feeling confused and scattered, fragile. It was a challenge even to answer the phone or return calls.

Frustrated by my lack of concentration and disappointed in my disorganization, I grew angry. I wanted to be reliable and effective again. As a result, I was overly critical and insecure, questioning everything I did. I expected more from myself, but felt less capable. Looking back, it seems like self torture.

Supportive friends and acquaintances would ask, "Did you read this book on grieving yet?" or "Have you had a chance to read your e-mail? I sent you a good poem," or "You really need to schedule time for yourself."

Time for myself? Though I had an army of people to help me, the demands of motherhood—changing diapers, emptying the dishwasher, rubbing bruised knees or soothing bruised feelings, changing wet bedding at 3:00 AM and giving hugs—made more strenuous with a grieving heart, left little energy to care for myself. But if the busyness caused me for a moment to forget I was grieving for Shawn, I chastised myself. The quest to strike a balance between grieving and functioning only served to further unnerve me.

In addition to taking care of my children were other duties such as running my household and organizing the events surrounding death, activities that lingered even months after the funeral. Because I felt so incapable, I dreaded going through all the new paperwork, sorting and sending mail, paying bills, getting gas for the car, changing light bulbs, programming electronic gadgets, fixing broken toys.

In grief's magnitude, I felt overwhelmed by tasks I knew how to do, or could have figured out before our lives were altered. Shawn used to do many of these things for me. And I missed those days. And it undid me to know I'd miss them forever.

The pink letter in the mail said, "NOTICE" in capital letters across the top. It was referring to an overdue electric bill.

When I called the company, the female voice on the other end of the line said, "You may have thought you paid it, but your bill is overdue."

I pay my bills online, and my bank statement verified the balance. "I'm confused," I said. "The bank deducted the money for the bill. I don't understand why it wasn't paid."

The voice informed me that I'd made only two payments in the past seven months. "The payment issues started when you moved in April," said the voice.

"I didn't move in April," I corrected.

"Well, the account was changed in April," she said while clicking on a keyboard.

"We've lived here since 2004," I told her.

"It looks like Shawn moved. That's when his name was taken off the account," she explained with a lilt in her voice as if to enlighten me.

The voice thought my husband was alive. Maybe separated—but alive. All I could say was, "Oh . . . uh . . . well, he . . ."

The voice said, "I see what's happening. All the bills are being paid on your husband's account instead of yours. If he doesn't live there anymore you need to change your account number."

I had called in April to say he was dead. It was time for the bills to come in my name. I didn't know the account number was changed. The tears stung hot behind my eyes. I had to tell the voice my story, and I was worn-out from continually having to relate my story to so many people. Why ruin someone else's day?

The tears rushed to the edges of my eyes but, in defiance, I was not about to cry over *an electricity bill.*

I quietly explained—*He was killed. Line of duty death. Two years ago. Please don't shut off my electricity.*

The voice was now regretful. "I'll put everything back in order. I've erased any late fees. It's all cleared up," she assured me.

I didn't have the stamina to correct her twice, but she was wrong. It wasn't all cleared up. A husband's death causes one misunderstanding after another. And sometimes it's too draining to discuss.

Grief can make daily life unmotivating. I lacked even the will to use our kitchen table, and fed my kids standing next to the kitchen island. I didn't feel like we were a family anymore. How I wanted to tell my kids, "Daddy will be home for dinner . . . let's ask him to read more stories then." Now it was just a mom and two kids, taking up space—using up time.

One morning while perched on top of a barstool, Jordan asked me, "When will we die, Mom?" He was four years old.

I wondered the same thing. Then for the hundredth time kicked myself for surrendering to my grief. "I don't know, Jordan. That's something no one knows . . . the day we die. What should we do today to make it special?"

"I want to play gymnastics." Jordan always has an idea.

Maddi jumped off the barstool with her brother and they practiced sommersaults on the living room carpet. I pretended to do a cartwheel, but couldn't get my legs up very high. I fell on my stomach, laughing. Jordan and Maddi piled on top of me. "Tickle! Tackle!" Jordan shouted, and a new game was born. We rolled around tickling each other until we were gasping for breath.

"I want to die, Mom," Jordan sighed.

"Why, honey?" I asked.

"Because I want to be with my daddy. I just want my daddy," he told me.

I couldn't blame him. It was a secret inside of me that I didn't share with anyone: I wanted to die too. I had no motivation to live because a life of unfulfilled desires accompanied by a mountain of bitter disappointments no longer seems worth living.

What did I need most? Food seemed to be furthest from my mind. Shocking loss impairs a person in all aspects of being—physical, mental, emotional, spiritual. And loss had taken a toll on me. I looked different, aged. When I looked in the mirror, I couldn't find the old me. It was difficult to believe that the old me even existed anymore.

> *It is also well to prepare a little hot tea or broth. . . .*
> *Those who are in great distress want no food, but if*
> *it is handed to them, they will mechanically take it,*
> *and something warm to start digestion and stimulate*
> *impaired circulation is what they most need.*

> —EMILY POST, *Etiquette* (1922)

Mechanical—Ms. Post was accurate in her descriptive word choice. I wondered if it was possible to disappear from the inside out. I felt emptied, and my body echoed with the pain of that emptiness. I craved to be touched by Shawn's love. My body felt guarded, neglected, and tense.

I didn't want to be an empty shell that merely functioned, covering up what was really happening on the inside. Hand me a little hot tea and I had no reaction. How could I expect anything else to revive me?

I didn't want to be around anyone who was happy or who appeared to be happy. Seeing families together at the store, at church, or in our neighborhood evoked memories of a full life—what life was like before Shawn died. Sometimes I would find myself paralyzed, staring. *How can they go on as if nothing has happened? Don't they know that my world*

has ended? These people have no idea of how quickly life as they know it can be over.

On January 30, 2006, I wrote:

> *I am not myself. I am overly emotional. I am newly*
> *unreliable. I am illogical. I am not thinking sensibly.*
> *I am discouraged and exhausted. My mind won't*
> *turn off. This is the darker side of grief.*

A few nights later some close friends called. "Hey, Jen, we're just checking to see how you're doing."

"We're okay," I lied, "just getting ready for bath time and early bedtime over here."

"Sounds good. We're making ice-cream sundaes and a fire to cancel out the cold. It's definitely a night to snuggle in," my friend replied.

I feigned interest, gave a weak chuckle, and explained I needed to round up my kids.

"Who were you talking to, Mommy?" Jordan asked.

"Who's dat, Mommy?" Maddi asked, trying to act as big as her brother.

"Just our friends . . . making ice cream," I rolled my eyes at why anyone would eat ice cream in the middle of winter.

"We want ice cream, Mom!" Jordan squealed.

"Me want ice cream!" Madelynn agreed in two-year-old enthusiasm.

"Well, it's bath time . . ." I began and then an idea came to me. "How would you like ice-cream cones in the bathtub?"

"Yeeeees!!!" the reply was unanimous.

You can make your night good too, Jen. Here was a much needed pep talk. I served my kids ice cream in the tub, with a smile on my face, still hurting and hollow inside but delighted for them. The teeter-totter effect of loss—continually balancing the ups and downs. *Why can't I allow myself to feel good? Will I ever feel good again? Why do I feel so stuck?* I was trying—or I thought I was.

I begged God to take me out of this life and place me elsewhere. Anywhere. Somewhere far from pain and misery, those robbers of life that had left me devastated by loss, stripped bare, and dead along the roadside. Crying out in desperation and sadness was becoming my new routine.

This wasn't me. Or was it?

Life had lost all joy; even reading books to my children became a chore. While I read the "Three Little Pigs," they'd point at the characters and scenery and chatter happily, and I'd think *What's the point of reading books? Why does it matter? What's the benefit? In the end we all die.*

Earlier in life I'd learned an Italian expression: "hang on even in the mouth of the wolf." I didn't know how to do that. Who was the wolf of death? Would he destroy my house like he had blown down my security? A simple children's book and I was distracted with philosophical questions posed by loss and pain.

I shared some of my tangled thoughts with my friend, Sarah, a psychologist by profession. We were roommates in college, and she had known Shawn long before we were ever married. She came to have dinner with me once a month after Shawn died.

"I thought depression meant I would stay in bed all day," I told her.

"It can," she said. "You can also be very capable of performing the daily tasks of life and be depressed. It's called *anhedonia*—the inability to experience pleasure from things one would normally find enjoyable."

In an odd way I felt relieved to have a diagnosis. Her description made sense. Activities at one time I liked to do—cooking, eating, strolling outside, watching a fun movie, listening to favorite music—now held little interest for me.

I functioned, but did not like it. I had some happy moments, but I was not happy. I was a walking textbook example of depression.

Many who are hurting almost beyond endurance try to avoid the pain of loss by ignoring it. I saw this as an option, especially to gain approval of those around me. I wanted to appear okay. But more than appearance, I truly wanted to find a contented heart. Some inner drive was, in fact, the only part of me that seemed to escape destruction. My pain made me stubborn—I felt determined to be a survivor, to engage in life. I wasn't about to let the wolf devour me.

One day I cleaned out my pantry and found receipts that I'd put off filing. Without thinking, I started to sort them by date. I threw away anything dated after September 6, 2005. Receipts for purchases made before Shawn died, I stacked neatly in a pile.

Without conscious intent, I knew exactly what I was doing. I needed to see what was important before that fateful date. What did we buy? What was worth spending money on? What did we value? Where did we store up our treasure?

I was particularly interested in the receipts from the month of August, only weeks before Shawn was killed. He'd bought an attachment for his camera nineteen days before his death. It was the last time he would ever walk into one of his favorite stores.

I bought brussels sprouts fifteen days before the accident. I'd served them with fish one night in an effort to be healthy. I hoped Shawn had liked it. Now I wish I'd made his favorite meal, beef Stroganoff. The same grocery receipt listed four small cartons of half and half. It was on sale, and Shawn loved it in his coffee.

A receipt from an out-of-town convenience store, dated exactly one month prior, reminded me that we were on the last vacation we'd ever take together. Twelve days before he died we bought egg noodles, and Shawn invented his own chicken noodle soup with vegetables from the local farmers market. The day before he died he'd made a trip to the hardware store with Jordan, the last errand he did with his son.

After sorting all the receipts, I stuffed them in a file. At first, I assumed this exercise only proved more profoundly the stark truth: Shawn was gone, and nothing else mattered.

Then I realized what those receipts represented: the treasure of ordinary moments.

This was the beginning of my life broken into moments.

True, the usual was no more. Nothing felt normal. Nothing felt ordinary. Yet once my life had been defined by the ordinary. Going through those receipts, I realized how precious and how full of meaning those simple and sometimes mundane moments had become.

I described these initial days of being mindful of my new normal as consistently inconsistent. My new habits without my spouse seemed intolerably uninteresting and therefore hopeless. I wished fiercely that I could go back to just one of my previous ordinary days.

I had no idea of where to begin redefining my life, let alone identifying how to create new meaning. I had God, my faith. Could I admit that I preferred my living, breathing husband, who I could see and touch, over my unseen, intangible God? *God, I cannot hide my heart. Everything is so different, so foreign.*

Like supper time. I craved the days when making supper was simply making supper; when making my bed would be a simple, mindless task, instead of an experiment in how long it took before I found myself slumped on the floor. I longed for days that didn't carry the weight of grief. If my new normal was to become a source of contentment in the ordinary—like I had before my loss—I'd have to find a way to make that happen.

With my idea for the ice-cream cone in the bathtub sprang other time-saving, mess-confining motherhood shortcuts. My kids started enjoying popsicles in the tub, even weekly dinners. We'd play restaurant. I'd make their plates of food and balance them on the edge of the tub. They loved it. And I didn't have to sit at a table sensing the void of their father.

I wanted these current days to feel as precious as the ones before Shawn's death, but I was extremely leery. I had experienced the unpredictability of tremendous change. What if I grew to treasure these new times, and they were taken away too? Or what if my new moments weren't as fulfilling? I felt like normal life and abnormal life were colliding, with me caught in the middle—wanting my old life and wanting a new life.

I kept coming back to the question, What is normal? Eventually I defined it as accepting what is in me and adjusting to what is around me. We can't deny our pain, we can't deny that we miss what is gone, but we can reason that if our former ordinary moments held meaning, so can our new ones.

But would I ever adjust to the new, let alone accept the pain from missing the old? And why did I feel like I was in such a different place?

One pastor described this feeling as *sacred space* versus *ordinary space*. Ordinary space is our old sense of home, our previous reality, our normal, status quo life. It's what we're accustomed to, the typical, habitual, and everyday. It steadies us.

The pastor taught that tremendous trauma can bring us into sacred space, a new home where we don't yet feel comfortable, where we see the world with new eyes, and question ourselves about what really matters. It's like having culture shock. Sacred space—with its unfamiliar territory and jolting new customs—distances us from our old world. It's a different plateau of existence, filled with significance. This is where I found myself.

For months after Shawn died, I felt like I was suspended between heaven and earth—not dead, but not quite alive. A continuation of the hollow place I initially entered when given the news of Shawn's death. It was uncomfortable, painful, difficult, but productive—there I sought worth, meaning, hope.

Waking each day felt like starting all over again. It took every ounce of my energy and resolution to live inside this new and sacred world. Each morning I'd put my feet out of bed wondering the same thing: *What matters? Is this really my life? Is there any meaning in today?* Quickly followed by a thought of defeat: *I don't want to do this.* Feet on the floor, though, the day had begun.

On Shawn's birthday, two years after he had died, I woke up, knowing the day had started backward. With covers over my head, I'd ignored my children's early rising. An hour after they'd been up I went to the kitchen. Sitting on the living room sofa, Jordan and Maddi were equal partners in a conspiracy. Peanut shells were scattered everywhere, on the floor, between the couch cushions—making a trail from the pantry.

"We're eating breakfast," Jordan told me.

"I see that," I said, my head dizzy from lack of sleep.

"Mom, what should we do today?" he asked.

"Today's your daddy's birthday," I announced.

Madelynn started to sing "Happy Birthday" in tune.

"Oh, I'm so happy," Jordan said.

"Yes, we're so happy," I sighed in exasperation.

Life had come and life had gone. In the sacred space, I now knew a secret that many seem to be unaware of: life is sacred. The knowledge of life's fragility can feel more like a burden than a blessing, though.

Life is *very* sacred.

Beyond this secret, I didn't know what to believe.

CHAPTER 5

The Grief Spiral

Love is the life of our heart. . . . According to it we desire,
we rejoice, we hope, we despair, we fear, we take heart, we
hate, we avoid things, we grieve, we get angry, we triumph.
—St. Francis de Sales

My friend, Liza, drove with her daughter, Summer, nearly two hours one Saturday morning to join us for a play date. My children were fascinated by our visitors. Liza had packed a variety of yogurts and granola to share with us. Guessing herself around my kitchen, she grabbed a plate to serve homemade muffins. As I watched her put the food on the table, I welcomed having someone else in charge.

Grabbing the butter from the refrigerator, she asked, "Can you describe the phases of grief you've gone through?"

"Well . . . some days I feel like I've gone through a twelve-step recovery program and still feel bad. Most days I feel like I haven't made any steps at all. It's more like circles of hurt that keep reoccurring."

As Liza put bibs on all the kids, her eyes told me she was listening and interested. This is the way conversations go between moms with toddlers—rarely sitting, inserting sentences between interruptions.

"And then on nights like last night, I dream about Shawn and wake up mystified. I still have to remind myself he's gone. I wouldn't call that a step. That's more of a downward spiral."

"I hope you put this in your book someday," she told me.

"Really?" I asked. It didn't occur to me that this could be at all helpful.

"Definitely. I think a lot of people—like me—think there are phases of grief you go through. But people who are actually going through it would be able to relate to how you describe it with the loops and circles."

My friend's perception was accurate. In grieving any profound loss, there is an array of emotions often mistaken as phases. Because grief is multifaceted, however, distinguishing grief by phases may be too simplistic. Each person experiencing loss will grieve in their own distinct way—following unique patterns. Grief cannot be predicted.

Psychiatrist Elisabeth Kübler-Ross originated a model to describe the five discreet stages of coming to terms with one's own imminent death: denial, anger, bargaining, depression, and acceptance. Some people have adopted this model to explain the process of surviving the loss of a loved one. But facing your own impending death is not the same as grieving a loss, and we all struggle in various ways to adjust to our own losses, even when we have little hope that we'll ever understand why they happened. As we grieve, we may recognize and process the Kübler-Ross stages, but they may wear different faces and identities, and may not occur in any identifiable series.

Another theory describes grief as a rise and fall process that includes times of shock, yearning, despair, and reorganizing toward a new life. With its many psychophysiologic components grief is better viewed as a cycle than a stage.

In the grieving world, I also discovered there is *normal grief* and *complicated grief*, which tend to correlate to the intensity and timing of death. When someone says, "My 90-year-old grandma died and lived a good life. I was sad, but at peace with her death," that is normal grief. Shawn's death was sudden, by murder, and provoked complicated grief. Complicated grief can last for years, and friends of the mourner may be surprised that grief is still present.

For me, those faces and identities of complicated grief came in loops, lassoing me without warning. I never knew when another face of grief would appear and what kind of sadness it would trigger. Maybe that's why many counselors describe grief as waves. It ebbs and flows. The strength of the tide varies, changing the intensity of the waves that break on the shore of one's daily life.

The tides of grief cause great variation in our emotions. I couldn't rely on passing through one stage and calling it complete. The phases I experienced occurred repeatedly and sometimes simultaneously. Some of the stages felt like my own invention.

Along with the waves came walls. I created barriers between myself and those around me or even within myself. A new kind of lonely fenced me in. When loneliness and confusion swirled together, the result was an even greater grief. Because now, along with losing Shawn, I was losing myself as well.

If I could have, I'd have built a barricade against the waves that swept over me. I would have welcomed Shawn back without a second thought. I would have traded in a heartbeat the wisdom I'd gained from the loss, saying, "Give me back my best friend." These were the lonely walls being constructed inside me.

January 11, 2006

Dear Shawn,

Today I am thinking about regret. Up until this point, I have felt blessed to say that I have few regrets about our relationship, our marriage, and our love. But today I am regretting many things. I am sorry for the times that I forgot to say, "I love you." I am disappointed for the times that I was too busy to kiss you goodbye. I am missing the times that I thought it was silly to hug you randomly for no reason at all. I am lamenting the times that I didn't encourage you and tell you how wonderful you are. I am guilty for the times that I forgot to compliment you, build you up and thank you for all you did for me. I am grieving the times that were wasted on things that didn't matter.

*Didn't we talk about this, Shawn? Didn't we agree
that one can never praise someone enough? Didn't we
discuss that sincere praise is the one thing that can never
be overdone? Didn't we decide that we would never get
tired of being built up by one another? We agreed that
we had never heard someone say, "Wow . . . I really am
overwhelmed by being told how great I am. It gets so old
after a while."*

*If I could have you back today, Shawn, I would
build you up. I would let you know that I believe in
you. I would tell you that you are strong and smart and
everything I need. I am sorry for all the times I skipped
my chance to let you know how much I needed you in my
life and loved everything you added to my life. You lived
what you believed, and I believe in what you lived. This
is a message that won't die quickly. I am breathing your
message. If I could have you back today, I would tell you
all about it.*

I heard it described to me that after a loved one dies, the survivor sees a
white wall. The white wall represents all the good memories of that loved
one. Some specks might appear on the wall, representing the loved one's
shortcomings, faults, irritations. But the specks are quite minimal, carrying little value in what we choose to recall.

I saw this white wall. I stared at it often, actually. I saw all the good
in Shawn and all the good he gave me. I remembered his weaknesses, but
even those seemed white to me, as I loved each part of him.

Around the corner of the white wall was a shadow—and that shadow
was me. I fixated on all the times I'd failed Shawn, the times I'd been
critical, disapproving, fussy, or unforgiving. I wished for one more day to
change things around. I thought, *This must be my punishment for living.*

I somehow understood, though, that this constant barrage of self-
reprimand did not restore my life or give me hope. It occurred to me

that I needed to reverse the situation: *What would Shawn have seen,* I wondered, *had I been the one who died and he the one who lived?* I think he would have seen a white wall.

Walking through loss brought feelings of abandonment and isolation. This is why the wave imagery in relation to grief works so well. Water and wilderness, shipwrecked on a barren island. Only those experiencing severe loss will understand the seclusion of being cast onto this island of sacred space.

I was lonely not from being by myself or from inactivity. The irony was that my days were filled with activity after Shawn died. Everyone who knew me was calling, taking me out for coffee, extending invitations. None of it, though, made me feel complete. At the end of each day, I was still filled with an indescribable sensation of searching.

I missed my spouse in every possible way, and, with all the people in my life put together, I couldn't replace him. Not because they weren't strong, good people—but simply because they weren't Shawn.

I wanted family dinners again. I wanted Daddy to come home and be a part of our nightly routine. I wanted phone calls from him and birthday songs and little notes and lots of kisses.

A month after Shawn died, I wrote my definition of lonely in my journal:

> *Lonely is the awareness of never again being able to ask*
> *Shawn what time it is. Lonely is the consciousness*
> *of now being the driver instead of the passenger.*
> *Lonely is the altered feeling of my children not*
> *experiencing Shawn's embrace. Lonely is the knowledge*
> *that Shawn will not be here to discern parenting issues*
> *with me. Lonely is the hopeless understanding that*
> *I will never kiss him again. Lonely is the wakeful reality*
> *that we won't have any more midnight conversations*
> *about our future dreams and ambitions.*

Lonely is sleeping without achieving rest, the fear of giving without being satisfied, and the dread of living without ever achieving contentment.

Not all days feel so desolate. But there isn't one day that I don't wish I could reverse the irreversible. Not all days are spent in isolation. But there isn't one day that I don't crave to share my life with Shawn. Not all days are solitary. But there isn't one day that I don't feel lonely.

I now faced a future of shattered dreams. I started a mental "supposed to" list: We were supposed to go camping that summer for the first time as a family. We were supposed to go to parent committee meetings together and wear matching school colors for our children's sporting events. We were supposed to grow old together and see what love looked like after fifty years.

I had lost intimacy, and it made me angry. I'd lost all the small, fun, silly elements of an endearing relationship. I'd lost my sense of how to be goofy, to not take everything so seriously. I'd lost all the would-have-beens.

One Saturday evening I found myself home alone with the kids in bed early. I didn't want to dedicate yet another night to being sad, so I made guacamole and poured a little wine. The two didn't mix well. I tried to think of a good memory to change my mood.

I remembered our first Christmas in our new home after returning from Honduras. That year I was big into traditions. I wanted to find a handful of things that meant Christmas just to us. Shawn helped me decorate the entire house. It looked like a winter wonderland—glittery cardboard snowflakes, an evergreen and pinecone wreath hanging in the entryway.

"Don't fall off the ladder getting that wreath up there," I said.

Tipping the ladder back and forth a bit he asked, "Like this?"

"Shawn! Don't do that!"

Shawn offered me his wide smile. "Okay, what's next?"

"Dinner?" Nursing Jordan, I was constantly thinking about food.

"Good. I'm hungry. Let's make coconut shrimp. It can be another tradition," he said.

"Perfect. I can already hear Maddi and Jordan someday telling their friends, 'Can't wait to go home and have Dad's traditional feast. Christmas isn't Christmas without his coconut shrimp!'"

Shawn had inherited his father's love for food made with island spices, and he enjoyed combining various recipes.

Hours later we were enjoying hot coconut shrimp by our new fireplace. A winter picnic.

The thought of all the should'ves made me not only angry but unutterably sad. And yes, depressed. And lonely.

Lonely is not something that disappears with time. In fact, as time progressed, my loneliness intensified. The silence of Shawn's absence was pushing me toward craziness.

Shawn,

> *I miss you in such ordinary ways.*
>
> *I miss you when my eyes open in the morning. I miss hearing you whistle and play guitar and singing me a made-up song. I miss holding your hand.*
>
> *I miss taking our kids to the park together or going for a hike. I miss driving places with you and how you always got us there on time. I miss even more getting lost with you and just driving until something looked familiar.*
>
> *I miss you in both loud and lonely times. I miss you when the evening is warm and I want to go for a walk in the dark. I miss waiting up for you. I miss you in the quiet of night when everyone else is sleeping—when I should be sleeping—when life is still and I want to hear your voice.*
>
> *I miss all of you—especially the parts I had yet to discover.*
>
> *I miss you in the simple things,*
> *Jennifer*

I was in the middle of what one counselor called "crazy-making," one of my own phases of grief in and out of sanity all day long. I'd see a picture of Shawn and he appeared real to me. A second look and I was thrown into a trance, wondering if what we had together actually existed or if my mind had played a horrible trick on me. Was he just an illusion?

One weekend when my kids were staying with my parents, I was home trying to figure out how to make a meal for one. I settled for a microwave version of Pad Thai and sat alone at our table to eat lunch. I glanced up at Shawn's empty chair and spontaneously started a conversation with him in my mind.

He began it: "What are we going to do today? What's on the agenda?"

His voice was clear and strong in my mind. He was sitting there, with me, enjoying the peanut-flavored noodles. Wearing a cotton T-shirt and khaki shorts, he looked like he had just showered and was ready to leave soon for his afternoon shift.

I considered our options. "I was thinking we could clean out the garage and find our hiking backpacks so we could go up to Taylor's Falls with the kids this weekend."

He took another bite and grinned. "Sounds good. I get off work early tonight. When I get home we can start on the garage and get ready for our hike tomorrow."

He looked content and relaxed. As long as I didn't stare too hard, he remained. I could smell his freshly washed shirt, and his arms were slightly tanned. It must have been summer.

"This is good Pad Thai," he said, talking around a mouthful.

I nodded and continued eating, satisfied with our plan and even more satisfied that he liked what I'd made for lunch.

I relaxed in the comfort of being appreciated. "Thanks. I'm glad you like it." I sent a gentle smile his way. "A hike would be nice. I haven't done that in almost a year. I really miss it."

My voice trailed off. I blinked. The image I'd constructed began to disappear. I was back at the table by myself. I could hear my fork clink against my teeth. *Since when do I pay attention to the sound of my fork?* In the stillness of the table, the silence of the whole room, my heart longed for another exchange with my husband, even if the subject was only a microwaved lunch.

I made a note to myself: I'm going crazy.

During one of our planned dinner nights, my friend Sarah brought over grilled chicken salads. Sarah was a great listener and I looked forward to our long conversations. She knew my history, so I could start all my stories in the middle.

Sitting down to eat she asked, "Do you ever just want to scream out loud?"

"I do scream," I told her, embarrassed but relieved. "It's just that no one can hear me. It's a silent scream. It begins when I wake up and continues through my day." I paused and took a deep breath, hoping she really wanted to hear all this. "I think I may even be screaming in my sleep."

Sarah broke her French baguette into pieces.

"It's the worst kind of scream because I can't get it out."

"Do you ever let yourself scream *out loud*?" she asked.

She was giving me permission, not asking a question, but I still wanted to answer.

"There've been a couple times. It scares me. I lock myself in the bathroom because I don't want my kids to hear me—or see me."

"Does it help?"

"Sometimes . . . I don't know—" I stopped. It was hard to describe. "Maybe . . . not really," I said, pausing again. She waited. I looked down, placing my hand on my chest. "The pain is always here; it doesn't go away. It doesn't matter if I scream or not. Screaming just helps the anger get out for a while. But it always finds me again."

I sounded so pessimistic—and I hated it.

My head dropped. I felt like I was in a confessional, exposed—guilty.

"A lady at church last week asked me if it's 'getting better.' I nearly broke down on the spot. I wanted to scream at her, 'Better? This will never be better!' When will watching my kids continually ask for their dad get better? When will wanting my husband back ever get better?"

My voice was trembling, a sign I was about to cry. I was so tired of crying.

"I can see why you wanted to scream." Sarah reached over and squeezed my arm.

"I'll tell you something," I said, continuing with my confession, "sometimes I want to scream at everyone. I feel judged by people who really don't get it. I cleaned out Shawn's sock drawer the other day just because I felt pressured by everyone asking me if I was moving on."

Sarah raised her eyebrows. "Only you know what's right for you. You'll find what it takes. This is about your timing."

"The sock drawer was actually uneventful," I said. "I thought I'd cry. I didn't. Maybe I don't have enough emotions connected to socks."

She smiled.

"Or to ties," I continued. "What does a person do with fifty men's ties?"

"You told me awhile ago you wanted to make a quilt out of his clothes," she said.

"Maybe I will. I like that idea—creating something. Or maybe I'll pack stuff away in bins. I really don't know."

I was tired. I'd spent so much time finding excuses for feelings I couldn't explain. "I'm not ready for this."

"What did you feel while you were going through the socks?" she asked.

"I felt guilty," I told her. Guilt—a phase of grief overlooked by Kübler-Ross.

Sarah sat quietly, her look steady, waiting for me to tell her more if I wanted.

"I felt guilty for cleaning out his side of the dresser. It felt selfish to use the space. Most of all I felt guilty that he died and I lived."

That's really why I want to scream, I thought.

The day after Sarah's visit, I stood gazing at our family pictures. One photo showed the four of us posing in the front yard. There we were, hanging happily on my living room wall. Here I was, miserably angry. Tears streamed down my face. The photo had been taken three days before Shawn died when we were still together and strong and connected.

"Why did you take that away from me?" I said out loud, not even sure who I was talking to. "Why is this happening? Why did we lose Shawn?"

The words echoed around the living room. No answer. Complete silence. I settled into it, let the resentment come over me.

Why do we ask "Why?" It's such an empty question. It doesn't take us anywhere. Are we impressed by the usual answers to *why*? That loss sharpens our character, makes us better people, or gives us a new glimpse of grace?

"Why Shawn?" I was entangled by this question and begged God to give me an explanation—to untangle me.

No point in telling myself I was just badly hurt, lonely, depressed. I was angry. I was very angry. I was mad at life, that it could disappoint so severely.

My kids stirred in their bedroom, and the noise shook me out of my trance.

Why won't they go to sleep? I demanded. I was agitated, my patience level beyond compromised. I'd been trying without success for over two hours to get them to settle down—nothing had worked. I wanted to take the happy photos off the wall and smash them on the floor.

I could hear my husband's voice in my head: "You're a good mother, Jennifer. Keep trying."

I wished he were standing in front of me so I could scream in his face, "I can't do this anymore!"

Instead, he won out with the last word: "If you wait until the point of losing it, then you've waited too long to parent. Discipline shouldn't be emotional. If it is, your parenting won't be effective."

"Well, Shawn, I've lost it. I'm beyond emotional," I yelled into the dark house. "You win!" I threw my hands up, a defiant surrender, and began pacing the living room. I rubbed my temples, failing to stop the headache that was forming. *What am I supposed to do?* Here I was having a fight with my dead husband and I still couldn't win!

The noise from the kids' bedroom grew louder. I crashed through the door and grabbed Maddi by the arm. She began wailing as I walked her forcefully to my bed across the hallway. I responded to her crying by biting my lower lip.

Jordan followed me. I turned around, picked him up roughly, causing him to start crying as well. He clung to me as I carried him to his room and dropped him back in bed. "Stay there!" My voice was raw with grief and anger.

I burst out in fresh tears. I wanted to give up. Why couldn't Shawn rescue me? Again there was the question *why* and me falling into the agony of the question once more. My mind didn't dare entertain the thought it had been holding at bay for months: *This isn't fair!* I knew, though, that fairness had nothing to do with it.

My kids sobbed in refrain, "I want Daddy!"

I walked back to the living room, bumped into the couch, then collapsed into it screaming, "Fall asleep. I need you to fall asleep."

"Mommy, stop screaming. Mommy, you are scaring me." I heard my son call from his room.

I stared at the wall, my vocal cords throbbing. I couldn't say another word. I was scaring myself. All I wanted was to find a way to jump inside that family photo, now hanging at a slant, another victim of my fury. I wanted us to be happy like the day we smiled for the camera, captured in contentment instead of now being confined by discontent.

Not knowing how long I sat in that position, I pulled myself up, walked around the house and turned off all the lights. My childrens' sobbing had turned into sniffling sleep. My best solution, my only solution, was to go to bed and start again in the morning. On my way, I stopped in front of the bathroom mirror and stared at the stranger who had replaced me.

"I'm so dissatisfied with life," I whispered to the reflection. "Don't you dare try to offer me an opinion. I'm disgusted with advice that doesn't work. Look at my eyes. I don't sleep. I'm dragging myself through life."

I looked away ashamed. It was one thing to be mad at the world, an entirely different thing to be mad at myself.

"Look at me! Look deeper. This is hurt at an ultimate level," I spoke louder now, "and this hurt is destroying me and my family."

I wanted somebody to understand. Even if just the ghostlike image in the mirror.

I wanted to lash out and hit something, but that might wake my sleeping babies, and even in my state I knew not to jeopardize the chance for some actual rest.

I shuffled from the bathroom to my bed and fell into a fitful sleep.

My friend, Andrea, called the next day and could immediately detect that I wasn't doing well. When we were college roommates, we'd sit on her couch for hours talking about life, young minds determined to figure it out. That morning felt like I was back on her sofa for a long chat. Only this time I wasn't expecting to solve life.

"The one thing that helps me sort things out and the one thing I am not doing," I told her, "is to write."

"Why aren't you?" she asked.

"Because I'm changing diapers and doing dishes and trying to remember to take out the trash," I replied. "By the end of the day there's too little of me left to make it a priority."

"What if writing became an assignment along with the laundry list of other things?" she asked, persistent with my comment that writing helped.

She continued, "Here's my idea, I'll call Ben and see if he can set up an online journal. If you want to post an entry, great . . . if you don't, that's fine too. But maybe if you think even one other person will read it and relate, it will give you reason to write . . . reason to put it on the to-do list."

Within days Andrea's husband, Ben, had added a blog to my Web site. And so I started writing everything out in detail: feelings, fears, disappointments, disbeliefs. Without knowing it, writing became a working therapy for me. I forced myself to write, even when I was tired. I preferred it over anything else, including sleep.

My counselor had told me disrupted sleep was an expected result of traumatic loss and grief. I knew that was true. I'd often stay up until one o'clock in the morning or later, journaling.

Most nights, though, sleep came easy, a welcome escape. Other nights sleep was evasive. As the anger deepened inside me, I wrestled with nighttime. One night I lay awake, repeating, *This cannot possibly be my life* until it became a chant. The clock on my nightstand flashed 3:11 AM, and I started to cry, becoming frantic. The sun would be coming up soon, and I needed at least two hours of sleep before my kids woke up.

I had a list of people who'd told me I could call them anytime, even at 3:00 o'clock in the morning. Now I needed just one person and I couldn't think of a single name. *No one really meant it anyway,* I thought bitterly.

I rolled over, trying to turn off the litany of fears, anger, and conflict. Continual thoughts—swirling. The lack of sleep was no benefit to my health.

Yet these sleepless hours contained a paradox; in the anguish of my new life, I met with the incomprehensible grief of losing my old life and began to chisel at the pain inside. I asked over and over *when will I stop hurting?* In my fatigue, I could feel God working in me, like a potter molding his clay. I prayed that God would give my new reality new meaning. It was sacred time, time I wasn't willing to give up.

Nighttime also served as a period of no obligation. I didn't have to answer to anyone. I didn't have to answer the phone or pretend to be happy or try to act like I was progressing through the stages of grief. I could be sad. I could miss Shawn. I could cry freely into the spiral of grief in my private nighttime sanctuary.

There are nights that the tears won't stop and other
nights when they seem to have permanently disappeared.
There are many different tears—
tears of sadness, tears of anger, tears of frustration,
tears of emptiness, tears of despair. The worst are
those that are all mangled together with every bit
of emotion mixed into the blend.

There are nights that I have more to write
about than actual time, and other nights I have
nothing to write about at all.

After crying awhile in front of my computer one night, I e-mailed my sister Deanna, hoping for some insight into my erratic behavior.

She e-mailed back almost instantly: "Give yourself permission to be this sad. How could you not? Your circumstance is heartbreaking. Let it break. You can't escape that."

She's right. There's no escape from feeling six emotions at once, from feeling crazy, from feeling the new normal. From wanting to scream out loud. And from wanting to scrap the rational stages of grief and yell, "Don't tell me where I should be!"

When he was alive, Shawn always told me "Don't worry about what other people think." He'd be the last person to place pressure on my grief journey expecting me to just get on with life. He'd be the first person to help me see that my life still has purpose.

But I didn't want to believe that his death brought larger purpose to my life. Could I even accept that my life was part of a bigger plan? Could I lead my children on this journey through loss to restored hope? How could I help them in the midst of my own hurt, anger, and doubt?

Most importantly, could I believe I was made to do just that?

CHAPTER 6

Tender Hearts

*Promise me you'll always remember: you're braver than
you believe, and stronger than you seem, and smarter
than you think.*

—CHRISTOPHER ROBIN TO WINNIE THE POOH

What's that there, Mommy?" Jordan asked, pointing to a tear on my face.

I couldn't speak.

"What's this one?" he asked again, pointing to another tear while wiping it away.

Trying to gather myself, I hoped my face showed love.

"There's a tear on your eye, Mommy. You sad, Mommy?" Jordan gently prodded.

I could barely nod.

Quietly he touched my face with his chubby toddler finger, and placed my teardrop on his own eye. "There's a tear on my eye, Mommy," he said. "I'm sad."

One of the harder things for me to deal with in Shawn's death is how it affects Jordan and Madelynn. Early on, I realized that their tender hearts were grieving along with mine.

My children . . . our children now had only me. They depended on me, trusted me to take care of them. Single-motherhood was an unfamiliar role, one I didn't know how to perform. Wanting the best for my children was a natural and automatic concern, but how could I give my best at a time when I felt constantly at my worst?

I'd never lost a father. How do I help my kids through something I've never experienced? How do I relate? How do I comfort? I wondered how I could help my children when I could scarcely help myself.

My counselor said I was in a state of overwhelm. Because they'd lost their dad, my devotion to my children intensified, but I knew that my being overwhelmed by grief was not a healthy state for taking care of an infant and a toddler. I feared that one day they'd say, "Mom, we didn't know our dad on this earth, but because of the devastation you carried, we never knew you either."

After this revelation, I knew it was vital to keep my mental health in balance. I was determined to provide a stable environment for my kids, but for them to heal, they'd need a healthy mom. And that meant that I needed to grieve Shawn as a wife before grieving him as the father of my children. The processes were linked, but distinct.

One afternoon after a park dedication in my husband's honor, a stranger approached me with condolences and said, "Don't get me wrong, I feel bad for you. But, who I hurt for the most is your children. They're the ones who have to live without a father."

I graciously accepted the words as I too felt torn apart for the loss my children were forced to accept into their lives. But I wondered why we have to compare grief and calculate whose loss is worse. It's not a competition. From every angle, loss empties a person. And I, too, wanted to be validated as Shawn's wife—a role I couldn't deny, a role that had once identified me.

Raising my children within these new parameters required delicate strategy. I needed to make sure that I didn't bury my own grief to attend to my children's, which could create resentment and hidden hurts for our future. Yet I didn't want to create an insecure and perpetually sad homelife, so I saved most of my tears for late at night. At times during the day I'd cry in front of my kids, but I didn't want that to be a habit. Often I'd barely make it through the day, then after my children were asleep, I'd retreat to my office to journal, working to conquer the pain inside.

I was deliberate about taking time for personal retreats outside the house, allowing myself time away from my kids. When alone, I didn't have to harness my grief, which often got pushed aside to fulfill my role as a mom. I could fully experience it without interruptions of children needing to be fed, changed, bathed, or waking up in the middle of the night. During my times away I felt God taking care of me as only a father can care for his child.

Jordan's and Madelynn's expressions are a carbon copy of their father's. They own his laugh and have inherited his smile. They mirror Shawn's traits. Jordan is inquisitive, bright, and tenderhearted. Maddi is affectionate, amusing, and determined. Usually a beautiful connection to Shawn, at some moments it's a painful reminder—a reminder that my children will never experience firsthand their daddy's personality and idiosyncrasies.

They will never again hear their dad's hearty laugh or feel his warm hugs. They'll never see him at football games, dance recitals, or graduations, won't hear his advice at the breakup of a first romance or job challenges, won't have him to celebrate weddings or promotions.

Ordinary activities with my children, then, are cast in a new light and take on new significance—watching a movie, ordering take-out food, playing at the park, goodnight kisses. I want to experience deeply each part of our lives together. Still, the void of a father figure is immeasurable, and I often ask myself, How do I fill this gap?

Once, before Madelynn was born, Shawn told me, "I have this sense that Jordan will endure something very heavy in his life." That was it, no details. So Shawn prayed over Jordan and Madelynn every night when he came home from work. He leaned over their cribs, hand outstretched, praying for God's protection and love in their lives. After he died, I started to do the same, but there's something deeply touching about a dad praying over his children.

I grieved for Shawn's loss. At least twenty-five times a day I'd long for my husband to see what our kids were doing. Not just see but participate in the experience. Some people had told me as a gesture of comfort that Shawn could still see us and was watching over us—like a guardian angel. Are souls in heaven engaged in what's going on here on earth? Could Shawn see that Jordan liked to climb trees and use his imagination? Did he know Maddi walked before she turned one and smiles with the dimple he gave her?

I don't pretend to know those answers. But I do know that Shawn loved being a dad, and while on vacations he spent many hours taking pictures of Jordan or wearing a baby sling with Madelynn on his chest. I wanted Jordan to hear his dad say, "Get your coat on," when we were getting ready to leave the house. I wanted Maddi to have her daddy help her put on her socks. I wanted our children to have their father on every outing, whether it was a trip to the grocery store or a holiday getaway.

I grieved that Shawn would no longer appear in beautiful family snap-shots, listen as his son learned to speak in full sentences, or enjoy slobbery kisses from his adoring daughter. I wanted him to feel the expressions of his children's love. I wanted to see Shawn interacting with his family as a living, breathing husband and father. I didn't want an angel. I wanted my kids to be part of a complete family portrait, with meal times and play times, not living in the thumbnail sketch that had taken its place.

This was my dilemma. I knew that Shawn was complete in heaven. I believe he is fulfilled and experiencing joy beyond comprehension. Still, I couldn't accept that his better circumstances explain why he was taken from us, why Jordan and Maddi now live deprived of those special, ordi-nary moments with their dad.

We never know when those moments will occur. During the last year of his life, Shawn had returned to school to study psychology and criminal justice, his goal to work with victims of traumatic crimes. One night he was preparing for an exam. Propped on the couch with books, highlighters, and class notes, Shawn had Jordan snuggled under his arm. I went to take Jordan, but with a grin he told me, "That's okay. Jordan's helping me read."

One week later Shawn was typing a paper for the same class. This time Maddi was nestled in his arms, relaxing with her dad as he worked at the computer. Again I approached him, knowing he could work faster without a baby on his lap. He insisted, "She's fine. She's helping me type. Leave her."

One week later Shawn was dead. How could that be better? How many special, ordinary moments will we miss?

Jordan and Madelynn would learn about their father only from those left behind, and ultimately from me. My only mechanism for coping with the magnitude of these thoughts was to tell myself, "Stay present in the moment and don't think too far into the future." Tomorrow would have its own worries, its own unpredictability. I found it safer to live only in the present day.

One Sunday a priest asked me how I was doing. "I hate to offer the cliché, 'just live one day at a time,'" he said, then quickly added, "Maybe it's better to advise those who are hurting to take life one-half of a day at a time, or more realistically the prayer should be, 'Lord, please help me to simply make it through lunch.'"

The next day was particularly stressful. At one point Jordan and Maddi both wanted the same blanket and were battling for it in a not very playful tug-of-war. I was hoping to just make it to naptime.

A prayer must have groaned in my spirit, "Lord, how can we make it through this moment?"

I snatched the blanket and put it over all of our heads. "Listen," I said in a hushed voice, "I have something to tell you."

They were captivated. "We're in a fort. Now snuggle close . . ."

My kids were in awe of this make-believe castle. We'd never played this game before.

"We're a team," I said. "Can you say that? Say 'team.'"

Now they were all ears and eyes—total interest.

They both echoed in unison, "TEAM!"

"Never forget that," I said. "We're in this life together and whatever happens, I will always love you. We will not give up on each other. That's what it means to be a team."

The blanket fort had worked. There was no more fighting. And in the process, I had made it through the moment. God was quietly teaching me, though I was slow to learn, that he with his fatherly wisdom would fill in the gaps I feared were left for empty.

Many people wanted to help and comfort me during this time. Along with help came a variety of opinions. A well-meaning acquaintance at church encouraged me, "God has a purpose in all this. It's clear that he wants you to be a single mother and to focus on your kids as you reestablish your life with them. I'm here for you as you embrace this new role."

I was hurt and confused, not because I entirely disagreed. But I was having a difficult time accepting God's "obvious" plan. I, indeed, wanted my children to have a stable life, wanted to be a good mother within the challenges of our situation. I just wasn't sure where to begin.

I wish I would have said, "Thank you. I'll never pass up help or support because that's one of the main ways God is sustaining me. I'm not so sure that God planned for me to be a single mom. All knowing, God knew what would occur in my life. And I believe he grieves with me—grieves that we live in a sinful, imperfect world where people die and hearts break."

My mind flashed back to Jordan's third birthday. While we were in the kitchen mixing batter for his cake, he said, "Mommy, my birthday cake is in heaven."

He then went to write a letter to his dad.

His sweet gesture only served to darken the day, giving him a sullen mom who couldn't stop sobbing.

Crying hysterically, I called Deanna. "I want Shawn to be here so bad for Jordan's birthday . . . Can you come over?"

"We were planning on it," she said.

I was glad I'd called her—someone who was good at calming me. As I waited for Deanna and her family to come eat birthday cake, one phrase repeated itself over and over in my mind: *I don't want to do this anymore. I don't want to do this anymore.*

I didn't know if I was talking out loud or to myself: *I don't want my children to celebrate birthdays, holidays, high points, or low points without their dad. Being a single parent doesn't seem to get any easier. The frustrations just get shoved away until there's no more space to push them in. And then the pain of loss shoots up, overflowing on all of us.*

On that day I realized a different type of milestone; for over a year now I had been living in pure survival mode. Each day I got up. Functioned. Moved. Didn't think about tomorrow. It wasn't a planned strategy, more of an instinctive method to keep going. I had once detailed out my days, now God was working his details in me. I had no interest in the plan. I could only concentrate on persevering moment by moment. Does God plan pain for our lives or does he allow it? I tend to think the ultimate answer is that he stands near our pain for us to know him more intimately. God can take the overflow.

In marriage there's a contract between two people to stick it out. Good or bad. I missed Shawn in his role as father, in both the fun times and the less-than-fun times. Single parenting is less than glamorous. I wanted "dad" to be the "preferred" parent—at least some of the time—because it was impossible being the only parent my children wanted. Another single mom referred to a dad as the "buffer parent," a kind of shock absorber for all the components involved with parenting.

Sometimes I didn't want to be a mom anymore. To clarify, I love my children and find great hope in them. But my concept of motherhood—with the ideal family of a dad, mom, and children—had been destroyed. My concept had, of course, been God's original concept too. In a perfect world, a family is supposed to involve Dad and Mom supporting each other in the assignment and ministry of raising children.

Shawn had been my best teacher in how to discipline calmly, play creatively, and work to communicate clearly. I loved talking to him about our children and learning how to be a better parent alongside him. Parenting is exhausting; single parenting can be grueling. When stamina is low it's hard to keep a strong interest in effective parenting techniques. Not only that, I felt insecure, not trusting myself to be as good at mothering alone as I had been with my built-in support system.

I could no longer just turn around, with Shawn jumping in to do the dad thing. He should be in the car with us, he should be at home after work, he should be giving the kids piggyback rides or baths or little life lessons.

Then I could be making supper, knowing certainly that the four of us would not be eating in the bathroom! He should be cooking with me and talking with me and joking with me. He should be listening to me, challenging me, helping me. Even disagreeing with me! I couldn't believe I missed our fights. But, even in our arguments, I knew that I had someone on my side.

The rewards and the trials of parenting often occur simultaneously.

One night at dinner, Jordan pointed to his chicken rice soup and said, "This is our mouse soup, Mom."

"Really?" I gulped, visualizing.

"Yeah. Maddi and I are mouses," he told me.

"I can see that," I replied. "You're both very sneaky."

Jordan and Madelynn looked at each other and giggled. Then, peering out the patio window, Jordan asked, "Is it still morning time?"

I knew exactly where this conversation was going. "It's not morning time anymore."

"But it's not nighttime either?"

"It's . . . almost . . . nighttime," I told him, wanting to put my hands over my ears.

"I don't want to go to bed!"

How many creative responses does one parent have to this protest? I was running out of originality. I needed Shawn. Then I was saved by a distraction.

"Mom! That's my daddy on the radio," Jordan exclaimed, forgetting his complaint. The man on the radio was singing and playing guitar, an immediate connection to Shawn.

To my son's dismay, bedtime did become a reality. As I tucked the blankets around my son's feet he said, "Mom, I'm so funny like my dad."

"Yes, you are Jordan," I told him, "and your dad loved to be funny!"

Turning to Maddi, I tucked her in the same way and blessed her on the head with a little prayer—our nightly routine. She kept asking for one more hug and some chocolate milk. An hour later, the stillness didn't convince me that my "little mice" were both sleeping.

Checking, I found Jordan sound asleep, both hands folded under his cheek. *One mouse down.* But his sister was sitting up in bed with an empty tube of menthol ChapStick, her head matted and sticky. Here was a chance to say something brilliant to enforce proper bedtime etiquette. I couldn't think of anything except, "That's for your lips," as if now was a good time to teach her how to use beauty products.

I scooped my little mouse up in my arms, brought her to the bathroom sink, and washed her hair for over ten minutes. Did you know that ChapStick, when mixed with hair, takes on an altered state, much like adhesive? And my daughter's entire head smelled like a store full of peppermint sticks.

Madelynn loved this late-night attention. As I carried her back to bed she started to cry, the cry turning into a full tantrum. Spread out, face down on the carpet, she flailed her arms and screeched, "It's not nighttime anymore!"

Ten minutes later she was fast asleep, still in the same position, and the whole room smelled cool and tingly. She was breathing deeply, her sinus cavities refreshed.

I went back to the kitchen to make some tea. I could relate to my daughter. Many nights I wanted to have a tantrum—many nights I did. Usually my outburst included, "I don't know how to do this!"

Parenting takes a sizeable amount of creativity, considerable patience and—more than those two combined—grace. Single parenting is an accurate name—the *single* most challenging thing I've ever done in my life.

Oliver Wendell Holmes once said, "Pretty much all the honest truth-telling there is in the world is done by children." But truth isn't always expressed just in words. How do babies, for instance, process and cope with loss? Do babies grieve? What can a toddler express about the loss of losing a parent? These were questions I asked every day. It was clear that my children knew something was strangely different, that their dad was absent, and that they missed him.

As a five-month-old, Madelynn's expressions were physical in nature. My easygoing baby, who'd slept through the night since she was three weeks old, began waking numerous times after I put her to bed. Our doctor suggested experimenting with feeding times and diaper changes, but finally made a direct correlation to grief. The sleep disturbance was Madelynn's way of conveying the loss her body felt but that she could not yet communicate with words. She sensed sadness in me, especially from breast-feeding, and the grief had invaded her.

After a year, she began experiencing night terrors. My aunt helped me study Maddi's sleep habits and worked vigilantly to find a solution. Maddi was two years old when I made this entry in my journal:

> *Maddi wakes up in a daze, panicking, looking to find*
> *me. Her body shakes with fear as I console her and bring*
> *her to sleep with me. I tell her she is safe and repeat,*
> *"I love you." She smiles sleepily and whispers back, "I wuv*
> *yuu, Mama." I wonder what is happening in her mind.*
> *I wonder what scares her. I wonder how to reassure her.*

From the moment Jordan realized his father had died, he began talking about the way he experienced it. At the time of the accident, he was twenty months old, constrained by a limited vocabulary. But as his word bank grew, Jordan shared more ideas with me. He wished with great passion that Daddy would come back. I often heard him calling out, "Daddy, where are you? Daddy, come here!"

Within a day after Shawn died, Jordan was questioning the absence of his father. "Daddy" was a daily topic. At first, his recollections and constant sharing astonished me. I started a baby journal and wrote down every time my children referenced their father, whether mentioning his name, pointing at a picture, or asking about the incident. This record of their phrases and actions will someday be a gift for my kids, for them to discover and find reassurance in the intimate connections they had formed with their dad.

Within weeks of Shawn's death, Jordan would accurately name Daddy's possessions within our home: Daddy's guitar, coffee, camera, pen, and police badge. One of his first three-word sentences was "Daddy fix it." He spoke correctly of his dad being "silly" and "funny." The most cherished memories revolved around bedtime routines. Jordan would frequently ask, "Jordan sleep Daddy's pillow?"

Jordan taught me early on that Daddy would be a figure he would incorporate into his daily life.

At times my children expressed their interest, curiosity, and love better than I could. My children had no inhibitions that limited their imaginations or hearts. Jordan and Madelynn were teaching me that it was okay to bring Shawn into a conversation. It was okay to miss him, it was okay to express our love for him, and most of all it was okay to remember.

The baby journal tracked the many instances that I hope never to forget. Eight months after Shawn's death I found Maddi holding a photo of our family. She was gleeful, pointing to Shawn, saying, "da da da da." I pointed to the other people in the family portrait, but she continued pointing to Shawn, repeating "da da da da," while her smile, sweet and gentle, widened across her face. She recognized him!

It took me a moment to find my voice. It was mixed with joy and regret. "Yes, Madelynn, that's your daddy!"

The way my kids expressed grief and loss depended on their cognitive developmental stage. When asked about his dad, two-year-old Jordan, for example, would point up and say "heaven." His references to heaven were location-based, as if Daddy now lived in Pittsburg.

At two-and-a-half years, when Jordan could actually verbalize short sentences, he would demand, "Daddy come down of heaven." It was a directional concept of logic—what can go up must be able to come down. When he turned three, the *why* questions began: "Why can't

Daddy come down of heaven?" "Why did Daddy die?" "Why is Daddy in heaven?" At three-and-a-half a form of reasoning began: "How did Daddy die?" "Why was Daddy hit by a car?"

The questions progressed as he matured, while my ability to answer waned—too many questions of my own. One time in the car, when Jordan had just turned three years old, he asked me, "Mommy, what did Daddy die about?"

I froze, with no good response. Was I to answer him with how Shawn died or with the cause for which his father gave his life? I answered both. "Jordan, your daddy was hit by a car. He died to save many people. He did an amazing thing, Jordan."

Nearly a year later we had another car conversation. Jordan told me, "Mommy, I want Dad to come down from heaven."

I answered, "Daddy can't come down from heaven."

Without a pause he asked, "Can we go up to heaven?"

"Someday," I said. "Someday we'll see Dad again in heaven, and that will be a splendid day."

Even as I explained this, I was unsatisfied. As a Christian I knew the theology behind fairness, still I considered it beyond unfair that a three-year-old would have to wait a lifetime to be with his father.

Jordan's questions deepened. "How did Dad get up to heaven? Does God have a rope?"

I replied, "Those are good questions, Jordan. Maybe God has a rope."

With this possibility Jordan asked, "Did God pull my daddy up? Did God use his rope to pull Daddy up to heaven? I think God uses his rope, Mom."

This is how the process went, gradually piecing together the bigger story. We talked about what we could handle and sometimes shared what we couldn't in an effort to mend and heal. Struggling hearts hold many questions for both adult and child. Instead of ignoring the layers of hurt, I felt the best response was telling the truth with present-mindedness—taking it one layer at a time.

Mothers want to provide safety and comfort for their kids. I hunted for resources that would help me to help my young children in their healing process. One question in particular haunted me: *How can I explain death to my little boy and little girl?*

Like undertaking a research project, I studied their grief. I noted their movements, sleeping patterns, behaviors, progress, setbacks, hurts, and joys. I asked counselors how to help my children but would often receive blank stares or at most a single-sheet handout with suggestions to review. Most resources were limited, and many inaccurate.

I found very little in reference to infant grieving. One counselor told me that babies won't feel grief or know anything of their loss until they are at least three years old. Other materials stated that children are unable to grieve until they reach four years of age. Still, my infant was clearly affected by loss. One Harvard study said that a baby as young as two weeks recognizes her or his father's face and prefers it over that of any other man. How could Maddi not sense a change?

A section in another book included tips for how to explain death to children. It encouraged the adult to tell the child that people usually die when they are *very, very, very, very* old, stressing the importance of *very* to indicate that most humans have a long life and live to an old age. The authors concluded that talking about death without the *verys* may be misleading.

Misleading? Misleading to whom? Misleading to a boy and girl whose father had been killed before either of them turned two? I understand that it's unwise to create fear in children about death. I can see that in order to bring a calming effect to the topic it's important to state that *most* people live long lives. I also believe, however, in the validity of being honest. From my children's perspective, the one who hadn't fallen into the category of "most people" was their dad—a very important person.

I found no other place to stand except in the truth of what had occurred: death comes to all ages. Shawn died young, and this was our hurtful, honest reality. At the same time, I was responsible to guard my children's hearts and share with them in doses what they could appropriately comprehend for their ages.

Jordan picked up his walkie-talkie that he had just gotten for his third birthday. I was standing by the kitchen sink, my back turned.

Jordan announced into the speaker very seriously, "Hi, Dad. This is Jordan. Where are you, Daddy? Are you there, Dad? Are you in heaven?"

Without turning around, I listened with interest. My son paused briefly, as if expecting an answer. "This is Jordan, Dad. I'm eating a banana. You're in heaven, Dad. Are you eating a banana in heaven?"

I couldn't resist peeking at Jordan and I grinned as I saw his happy smirk.

I believed this was only the beginning of a lifetime of conversations Jordan would share with his father. Although abstract in form, his chat was refreshingly straightforward. Children possess the gift of speaking what they're feeling.

Nine months prior, Jordan had called out from our kitchen, "I want Daddy. I want you, Daddy. I want Daddy. I want you, Daddy." There was fervency in his voice.

"I know, Jordan," I told him. "I want Daddy too. I know, Jordan."

"No!" he screamed. "You don't know! I want my Daddy."

I thought I could relate, but my son had told me otherwise. His grief was his own, and I made a mental note: *From now on, simply listen.*

A second round of pleading began as Jordan repeated, "I want Daddy. I want you, Daddy. I want Daddy."

His tears fell as the recitation continued for well over five minutes.

He grabbed his favorite blue and red blankets, offering them to me as he wept. "Hold you Jordan, Mommy."

I gathered him in his blankets, grasping for any way to connect and comfort.

He grabbed hold of me and tightly clenched his fists, calling out, "I want Daddy."

That was all he could say. That was enough.

I held my son, stricken by the tenderness of his heart, felt his little body collapse in sadness. *How do I hold his pain? I can hardly touch my own. How can I make things better?*

As we rocked on the floor, I realized that my little boy's feelings had been bottled up for over five months, waiting for his vocabulary to catch up with his heart. He'd finally been able to share his feelings with someone he trusted. He'd finally verbalized what he'd lost and what he wanted back.

Just as I needed to journal to express myself, Jordan needed to verbalize his sorrow. This to me was proof of the importance of language. Child or adult, we cannot heal without some form of articulation, whether in words, writing, music, or phone calls to friends. Jordan's expression that day was pure, raw, innocent, loving, sharp, and clear. It was authentic grief.

I was comforted in my belief that this little boy was going to be okay. He would learn various ways to cope with such a tremendous, irreplaceable loss.

Several months later I observed a coping strategy Jordan was using by outlining the framework of his dad's death in his mind. He was finding what loss therapists would call "context," a way to categorize his loss. We were riding in the car, and by now Jordan's vocabulary had expanded significantly. He looked at my eyes in the rearview mirror and asked, "Did Daddy get hit by a bad guy?"

"Yes," I said.

"Did the bad guy hit him in the face?" Jordan asked, wanting to figure out why he didn't have a dad anymore. Madelynn was watching her brother—silent but curious.

"No," I replied.

"Where did he hit him, Mom?"

"In the back," I said, briefly. I didn't want to lie, but I did want to protect.

"And then they threw the bad guy in jail?" Somehow my son knew the story, knew that there'd been some measure of justice exacted for his loss.

Maddi, being younger, had her own way of putting her loss into context. Shortly after she turned one, she began to play with her dollhouse. She'd put the mommy doll and grandma doll in the house together, often avoiding the daddy figure.

A play therapist explained to me that children use playtime to figure out the world around them. Play is a way of self-discovery and interpretation. The roles in Madelynn's world had been changed, and she was working to make sense of who now took care of her in place of her dad.

Over time her play incorporated what she was noticing—from storybooks or other families outside our home, as well as photos of Shawn throughout our house. When she played, she gave everyone a title. Madelynn would point to herself saying, "Me. Mom." Then she would point to me proudly and giggle, "Da-da, Daddy."

I'd ask her, "Do you want me to pretend to be the dad?" and her face would light up with satisfaction that I had interpreted her message correctly.

On Father's Day we were driving to church to bring balloons to the cemetery. This was our new tradition for special occasions such as Shawn's birthday and the anniversary of his death. Sometimes Jordan and Madelynn would draw pictures or scribble messages on the balloons and we'd release them to heaven, sending up our love. Other times we kept some of the balloons for home as I discovered preschoolers don't like to let go of balloons!

On the drive, Madelynn was trying to get my attention.

"Mama. Mama? Mama!" Madelynn repeated with such frequency and volume I could hardly respond.

"Yes, Madalina, how can I help you?" I interrupted, calling my daughter by one of her many nicknames.

"I not 'Madalina'—Mamalina!" she told me, inventing a nickname for me.

"Madelynn, you're being funny," I said.

"Golly wolly," she replied with a hearty belly chuckle.

"Madelynn," I told her, "you laugh like your dad!"

Jordan perked up, turned to his sister, and said, "Maddi, my daddy died on the cross with Jesus. I'm really sad I don't have a daddy anymore."

I looked in my rearview mirror to see Madelynn listening closely to her big and all-knowing brother.

Jordan was used to an attentive audience and kept sharing. "I really miss my dad. I miss that I didn't need him anymore . . . But Mommy didn't die, Maddi. We must have a mom because we might need a mom."

Arriving at the gravesite, Jordan's arm started bobbing up and down pointing at an American flag. With fervor in his voice he called out, "Daddy's cross!" Ever since the funeral he had named the American flag, *Daddy's cross* or *Daddy's flag*. This was the last memory he had of his father, a casket draped by the flag of our country.

We got out of the truck and let our balloons soar.

Later that night at dinner, my kids ate macaroni and cheese with hamburger added in as an experiment. It had been a full day, leaving little time to be creative for supper.

"I don't like it," Jordan said. He wasn't shy about offering his opinion.

"Well, this is what we're eating tonight, and I'd like you to be appreciative," I replied.

"I wike it, Jo-dan. It good!" Maddi said in a positive Pollyanna voice, trying to convince her brother.

One out of two isn't bad, I thought.

I wondered what Shawn would have said when his son didn't like what Mom had cooked for dinner. Without warning, a few tears slipped down my face.

Madelynn instantly noticed. "You sad, Mommy?" she asked.

Kids are so aware. Even when we think they don't see or hear, they do. They get it.

"A little," I told her.

Without prompting, Jordan's eyes welled up and he said, "I miss my dad. Mom, hold me."

I immediately felt bad. By this time I rarely broke down in front of my kids. I don't believe in hiding my grief, but I also don't need to cry in the macaroni. I let Jordan sit on my lap for a minute, and then we had a group hug. The sixty-second embrace brought back some smiles.

One thing I feared after Shawn died is that my kids would not grow up to be who they were meant to be. How could they develop and grow and learn without their dad? It would be like half of them were missing. But, shortly after Shawn was gone, God gave me an unspoken peace that told me my children would grow up to be strong people. Character traits such as grace and honesty, independence, leadership qualities, integrity, the ability to communicate feelings and show compassion for others were all strengthened in them as a result of their loss.

My children were growing up to be exactly who they were meant to be, under God's guidance, helping each other and realizing we were in this together.

One night, long after I'd tucked my kids into bed, Jordan called out for his dad. When I looked in, his many treasures were scattered on the bed. Part of Jordan's bedtime ritual included a scavenger hunt to find exactly what he wanted to sleep with each particular night.

This night his bed was filled with kitchen utensils: a spatula, a soup ladle, a lobster cracker, and a whisk—transformed into either tools or weapons. In one corner of his bed lay a small photo album I'd put together after Shawn died. It was filled with photos of my kids with their dad.

Jordan caught me taking inventory of his stuff. Nonchalantly he looked away.

"I want to sleep with that," he told me.

"That's fine," I said.

"Hold me," he replied.

"What's going on?" I asked.

"I'm sad, Mom," he explained. "I want you to hold me with my feelings." I was positive that my four-year-old knew more about feelings and what to do with them than many adults.

Glad to comply, I scooped him up in my arms and rocked him while standing.

I posed a question I'd never asked before: "Jordan, if your daddy could come back and you could tell him anything you wanted, what would you like to say?"

It seemed as if he'd thought about this question before. "I would say,

'Daddy—I miss you. Please come back and take me up to heaven. I want to go to heaven with you.'"

The day came and passed. I'd marked the date in my mental calendar, but had forgotten to acknowledge it. I needed to call Deanna.

"I forgot an important date," I said without even saying hello.

"Hi," she said. "What did you miss? You don't sound very good."

"Yesterday," I told her. "I missed yesterday. Madelynn turned the exact same age Jordan was on the day Shawn died."

"Oh," she replied. The kind of "oh" that said she understood this was really bothering me, but had no idea what to say.

I reasoned that numbers didn't matter. How could I quantify all the love that Jordan had absorbed from his father in twenty brief months? Five fleeting months was my calculation of the affection Maddi had bundled up inside of her as a treasure from her daddy. Exactly 150 days.

"Are you still there?" my sister asked. "Are you okay?"

"Dee, she was just a baby! She *is* still just a baby. Jordan was just a baby. Babies! Do you hear what I'm saying? How do I begin to interpret loss for them? How do I measure it? No matter how I work it out in my mind, he's gone and they're at a loss!"

I felt like slamming the phone into the wall, felt like walking out of the house and not coming back until something made sense.

"Never mind," I said. "I'm talking in circles. I don't know why I counted backward on the calendar anyway . . . it doesn't matter."

"But it does," Deanna told me. "I'm sorry, Jen."

"I know." I said goodbye and hung up.

As my kids grew, the timeline seemed to carry us farther away from our life with Shawn. I continually calculated variations of days backward, forward, or in any direction, waited for certain dates to occur and pass so that I could associate the occurrence of trauma with periods of time. My children deserved more days with their dad. I didn't want my kids to miss out. I didn't want Shawn to miss out. Most honestly, I didn't want me to miss out.

How could life be good again with a key person missing from our family? At the same time, with one glance at my beautiful children, how could I refuse to find the good? I tossed the argument back and forth in my mind with no real resolution. My dread of the future was robbing me of joy in the present.

I'm intrigued by how many significant conversations take place in cars. Shawn and I used to have some of our best conversations on long road trips. Once en route, there isn't much chance for escape. With Jordan and Madelynn strapped in car seats, we find many uninterrupted moments to talk about our loss and explore how we are feeling.

Jordan was looking out the car window when he said, "I want my daddy." Madelynn was looking at me. I was a captive audience.

"You know, we can talk to him any time we want," I said. "We can talk to daddy in heaven, and I believe he'll hear you." I'm not on solid ground with my theology here, but I was desperate to provide my kids with something that would help them.

Jordan's face lit up, and he waited to see what I would do.

"Dad . . . Shawn . . . we just wanted to say we miss you," I said, my voice on the loud side, faltering.

"Mom," Jordan told me, "You don't have to shout. Talk to him nicely."

I guess I didn't know the volume to use when conversing with heaven. "Well, you both can try it if you want," I told my kids.

Madelynn giggled pleasantly as she said, "Hi, Daddy."

"I miss you, Dad," Jordan said. "We're going to the park today." A bit quieter he said, "Please come home, Dad."

My kids took out some picture books from the seat pockets in front of them. I concentrated on the road—that and on one sentence that slashed through my mind like the white lines dividing the highway lanes.

I hope I'm doing my part.

One weekend I took Jordan and Madelynn to an indoor water park with my sister Sarah. My kids were intrigued with the enormous slides and water toys. They splashed and giggled and counted to six before jumping into the water. I loved their joy and that they were so good at not allowing the cares of the world to bother them.

I, though, immediately noticed both dads and moms at the park, taking turns chasing energetic little bodies around the edges of the pool. One dad kept going down the waterslide with his little boy on his lap. Never seeming to grow weary, over and over and over the dad would go down the slide with his son. My heart sank, wanting my children to experience the same.

The loneliness of single parenting again crept in. *Will I be enough for you, Jordan? I know I'm not asked to fill your father's shoes nor could I ever accomplish that feat. But will I be enough? Will I be good at going to water parks and camping and taking you on vacations?*

Will I be enough for you, Madelynn? Will I be the one you can turn to when you're scared? Will I be the one who can teach you new things? Will I be the one who is strong even when I feel unsteady? Will I be enough for you?

Many times I felt safer at home, where we didn't have to compare our life journeys with those of others. Then again, I knew we could stay inside only so long before that, too, would swallow us. In or out, both were frightening.

Regardless of feeling intimidated, I sensed a necessity to keep moving—keep trying. *Move into your fear,* I heard from within. *This is where you will breathe again or at least believe there is reason to.*

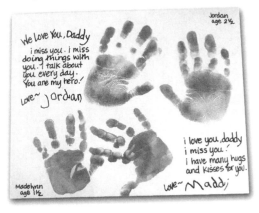

PART THREE

HEALING

*The north star is a star in the sky that is constant,
unwavering—a guide. I pray this is what we will
be to each other in our lifetime—constant, faithful,
unwavering, steady, quick to forgive, full of love—
guiding each other to our next life with our Creator.*

FROM JENNIFER'S ANNIVERSARY LETTER TO SHAWN
May 12, 2001

CHAPTER 7

Move

*The pain never goes away so you have to start moving
and working with it.*

—NANCY KELTON

When Jordan was just a little over three years old, he tiptoed to my bed one morning. With his nose near my cheek, he asked, "Mom, should we wait until the sun comes up to say 'good morning'?"

Squinting through one eye, I read my alarm clock—6:02 AM. Not yet conscious, I rolled over and thought *Yes, wait for the sun.*

"I know how to get to heaven, Mom," Jordan said, not relenting.

"Really?" I asked. Now I was wide awake.

"Yes! You fly there," he said. "I can fly there up to the clouds just like Superman or Batman."

"Wow," I told him, "that's good to know."

"Yep," he said, "that's how you get to heaven."

Tugging at my arm, he persisted, "Wake up, Mom. Let's get into the morning."

As I crawled out of bed, his words stuck in my mind. *Get into the morning.* What did that mean to me? It had powerful imagery—put effort into my day, face it, deal with it, live it, breathe it, learn from it . . . move with it.

I needed to start moving. After all, life is about movement even though it had lost a lot of the light I'd moved by. I stood in front of my bathroom mirror and told myself, "Move, Jennifer. Just move. All you need to concentrate on is moving." It's a boost, especially when the morning itself feels inconsolable.

Move, I thought. *In God we live and move . . .* Was this my new instruction for healing?

Later that same day, Deanna called to ask how I was doing.

"I'm considering a job at the zoo," I said, only half joking. "But that'll have to wait because I'm making lunch for two adorable monkeys right now—so adorable they decided to decorate their bedroom walls with a yellow marker!"

Deanna promised she'd call me back during naptime.

"I'm writing," I told her.

"Are you feeling better than earlier?" she asked.

"I still feel bad," I said, "not about the marker thing—that's the least of my heartaches. I just don't feel motivated to do much of anything."

Deanna doesn't say much when I need to philosophize; she just lets me talk.

I continued. "I found a piece of paper tucked in my dresser this morning. It said, 'I hate life.' I don't remember writing it. I just kept staring at it—wondering, *Is this really me?*"

"You're hard on yourself," my sister told me.

Heaving a long sigh, I went back to my original topic. "Anyway . . . writing helps me sort out the heaviness . . . so I figured it couldn't hurt."

"Hmmm," she said.

"I decided I could write and be sad . . . or I could sit on the couch and be sad."

"Good," she replied. I could tell she was thinking.

"Writing is a good listener . . . it's a constant," I told her. "When I make time to write, it makes time for me."

"Interesting how it seems to have worked," she said.

"What do you mean?"

"Well . . . even though you didn't feel like it, you did what has always felt satisfying to you. You made an effort—not simply filling your time with busyness, but rather with meaningfulness. Writing appears to be your therapy."

After she hung up, I mulled over our conversation. *It's a lonely place to be stuck in hate,* I thought. *Maybe that's why I wrote that note just to myself.*

My main conclusion? I can't trust my feelings. My feelings are valid, but not always reliable. They differ so vastly from hour to hour. What seems hopeless in one moment can be hopeful hours later. The comment about working at the zoo is a case in point. At that moment I wanted to find a way out of my mess. But did I really want to run away? No! I want to experience a real, engaged life with my kids. I want our lives to be filled with love and contentment and hope.

I need, then, to trust what I know instead of what I feel. One thing I know is that God gave me a passion to write. So I trust God to use the writing to move me through the grief toward hope, to move me—regardless of the hopelessness surrounding me.

I'd played piano and sang since third grade. Shawn and I joined the worship team at church while we were dating, and played with the group for over four years before our time in Honduras.

About nine months after Shawn died, our friends Paul and Lisa caught up with me in the church parking lot. Paul sang with the band and had sung at Shawn's funeral.

"Hey, Jennifer," Paul called to get my attention. Looking up, I saw him and Lisa waving.

I tried to wave back but both hands were in use by Jordan and Madelynn. As I lifted my kids into the truck and started fastening seat belts, Paul and Lisa walked over to see if they could help.

"Molly's taking maternity leave for a few months," Paul told me. "Our director, Sue, is looking for someone to fill in. What do you think?"

"I don't know if that's such a good idea." It was my way of saying *no.* The idea of playing for mass seemed like a setup for disaster.

After Shawn died I continued going to church, but could barely get through the service. Our faith had been one of the most intimate things we shared, and sitting in a crowded church without Shawn made me feel like a fly caught in a web—insignificant, helpless, trapped. Falling apart in the back pew was one thing—crumbling in front of hundreds of people with a microphone in my hand was something I didn't want to test.

"Well, you know we'd love to have you back any time. We all miss you," he said.

"I'll think about it." I gave them a weak smile.

"Okay," Paul said, "but one more thing, and then I promise to leave you alone." A brightness lifted his voice. "Just think. You already know all the parts."

"And I'll sit with your kids during mass," Lisa added. "We've got you covered."

Later that week a message waited on my answering machine: "Jennifer, this is Paul. I thought of something else. What do you think of singing with us for just one Sunday? A 'see how it goes' kind of thing? No pressure. Just an idea."

More than an idea, it was support in the form of gentle (and a little bit persuasive) encouragement. It prompted me to move, to do something. I went to practice the next week for my "trial Sunday"—and stayed on as a full-time member.

This time at church, instead of feeling confined, I felt protected. The moment I walked into my first rehearsal, I felt like I was coming home. I was welcome. My friends provided a safe place for me to be myself—all parts of me. Once a hobby, music was now a source of hope and healing.

My musician colleagues greet me like family.

"Hey, Jen," Dan on bass guitar calls out. "Good to see you." Clyde tests my microphone for a sound check.

Steve, on electric, nods; Darren and David, on acoustics, wave between strums. Mary looks up from the piano. Molly pats my shoulder, and Sue throws me a smile while directing each downbeat.

After a few months with the band, I even wrote a song. Our group taught it to the congregation and used it periodically for worship.

I drove home one night after practice in the first snowfall of the season. The flakes sprayed into my headlights like fireworks. I thought about the other musicians, our friendship, and the new song I'd written—all things that kept me moving.

Hanging up my jacket in the entryway, I noted a familiar hush, which had evidently moved in. My kids were having a sleepover at my mom and dad's house for the night. I sat down at the piano and took out my sheet music. Grabbing a pencil, I changed a couple chords. I let my fingers run over the white, smooth keys, repeating the chorus several times until I couldn't see through the blur of tears.

"What does it matter, God?" I asked, looking up at the ceiling. The house became stark with silence again as soon as I stopped playing. "What does it matter what I call it: doing, moving—healed, healing? None of it makes me better."

None of it changes how much I miss him, I thought. This time I wasn't talking to God. But I'm sure he heard, because as I walked down the hallway toward my bedroom, something inside me told me to keep writing, keep asking, keep trying, keep wondering—keep moving.

Something inside me said, *Yes, Jen—it does matter.*

One of my new friends, Chanttel, was a widow who had recently remarried. We met for lunch about once a month after Shawn died. During one of our get-togethers she told me, "Jen, healing is really hard. A new relationship doesn't mean the loss of the first doesn't hurt."

I stared at her, knowing this is why I liked her so much; she was real with me. I looked to her as a mentor, as someone who was successfully working toward wholeness.

"Don't get me wrong," she said. "I love Jeremy. He's my daily blessing. I just know that I have to continually work at the healing process just like I have to work at my marriage or raising my kids. It'll be a journey I'm on for a lifetime."

"How do you keep going?" I asked.

"Baking," she said.

I laughed.

"No, I'm serious," she told me. "You write. I bake. I made so many different kinds of cookies after Tom died that I had to start throwing them away. They were overtaking my freezer, and I could only bring so many to the kids' baseball practices."

"So . . . you're telling me the key is to do something," I said. "I've sort of figured that out, but I'm not sure it's made a lot of difference."

"You have to keep going," she stressed. "Remember that other police widow we met at the C.O.P.S. meeting, who volunteered in Zimbabwe?

"Mozambique," I corrected.

"Yes! I think the best therapy is to find what you like to do and do it."

"And if you don't want to?" I asked, stirring my lemonade with a straw. My friend's expression changed as she stared at me.

"Jennifer . . . our lives can become death, or death can be one part of our lives. We choose."

Moving doesn't, of course, make everything okay. The expected reply to the question, "How are you?" is, "Fine." But I knew I wasn't fine.

I'd been shaken by a recent letter from a close friend telling me it was time to "let go" and "move on." Many suggestions for processing grief. Not so many solutions. I was confused by these terms. They made no sense to me. Hadn't I already been forced to "let go" of my most treasured friend, my husband, and my confidant?

I cringed at the phrase, "moving on" as it neglected to consider the heart of the one hurting. The expression insinuated that I wasn't in a good place to begin with, before Shawn died, and now that he was gone I could find a new location or lifestyle. As a method to heal, "moving on" pressured me to get over my grief or ignore it. I'd wonder, *Move on to where or what?*

I also connected the idea of "moving on" with a certain pace. To me, it suggested I wasn't grieving fast enough—basically it said, "hurry up and heal." The message to "move on" or "let go" suggested that the quicker I could do this, the earlier the pain would disappear.

I believe the idea stems from a world of drive-through Happy Meals, quick cups of coffee, and instant Internet delivery. We want fast fixes for everything from buying a furnace filter to healing a broken heart. The world wants us to be happy because it does not know what to do with the sadness of grief-stricken pain—it does not know what to do with heavy questions that aren't accompanied by easy answers or quick solutions—a world that thinks this is all there is, that doesn't recognize this life as temporary.

I'm not certain I will ever say I'm "healed" in the sense of past tense. I believe my loss will always be a part of me. If I live to be eighty-nine, I'll be just as mystified about why any of this happened as I am now, a young widow raising two children.

My best hope is to say God is continually at work in me. Healing is a continuum. Aren't we all really on a healing journey—from something— until we meet our Creator?

After living through a very public and eventful year, including an invitation to meet the president of the United States in Washington, D.C., and a complicated trial process, I welcomed the relative serenity of a year or two to meander on my own private path to rebuilding. But quiet doesn't take away the hurt either. In many ways, the pain becomes more evident when there isn't as much to distract it.

That's one of the truths about grief—it's possible to ignore it, but that doesn't make it go away. We can try to handle it, package it up, put away old photographs, box up the clothes, but the funny thing is—grief isn't practical. Grief has its own method and mind. I've lost count of the times I found myself putting something away, in order to appear like I was "moving on," only to be lost in a memory while folding Shawn's shirts, with fresh new feelings as if he had just died yesterday.

Mark Matousek interviewed author Joan Didion, who at the age of sixty-nine lost her husband. "You don't actually get over things," Didion said. "They become part of everything you are. This does not mean you walk around crying all the time. But you change."

I was changed. I'm different now. And "letting go" or "moving on" could never undo that change.

Healing would not automatically occur through a career change or a new house, or by the opposite—doing nothing. Something we all have in common in relation to healing is that healing takes concentration and intent. Healing is hard work.

Through counseling I learned there are two types of grieving: emotive and instrumental. Emotive grief often takes an internal approach to the healing process by focusing on the emotions caused by loss. It tends to be a more private or inward way of grieving. By relying on language to express our feelings, we identify our emotional state and attitudes toward grief, and define a new view of reality based on those feelings. Counseling gave me a place to put my emotive grief, to talk out my thoughts and hurts and to work on my point of view.

An instrumental style of grieving seeks meaning in the loss through action. I knew my primary style was instrumental. The only way through my pain was to find something constructive—like writing or music—to grasp onto in the middle of this whole experience until I could make something that matters. I focused on action, which in turn also brought new insights.

The idea of connecting action with my grief dovetailed with my quest to *do something*. I needed to work *through* my pain instead of striving to outrun it. Finding worthwhile reasons to keep going and trying new things helped me to absorb my loss. As I recognized each symptom of grief—such as hopelessness—I faced it, then moved.

Andrea called on her commute to work one morning to check in with me.

"How are you doing?" she asked, "I haven't heard from you in a couple of days."

"I'm here. I'm just glad to be moving," I told her, honest and bordering on hopeless.

"That sounds like all that should be expected," she said.

"It's just hard to find anything I'm really interested in without Shawn," I told her. "It takes a lot of effort and still doesn't seem to make that much of a difference in how I feel."

"You expect a lot out of yourself," she replied.

"Are you sure?" I asked.

"Well, let me put it this way . . . I'm just glad to hear that you're not in bed with the sheets over your head. Jen, I'm proud of you," she said.

"Really? Proud?" I asked, incredulous.

"Yes! *Moving* is a big accomplishment. In fact, *you* encourage *me* to find at least one thing a day to do that matters. It's easy to become complacent. I think that's what happens to a lot of people. I can't imagine adding grief to doing nothing that matters."

"There's a lot of thickness to move through with grief," I said. "My neighbor asked me today if it's getting easier."

"And what did you say?" she asked.

"I just said something like 'I'm growing more accustomed to it,' and admitted I don't know if it'll ever be easy. I really wanted to throw up."

It sounded like Andrea was choking on her latte. "You know that lady was just trying to find something to make you feel better."

"Or make herself feel better," I said.

"People don't know what to say," Andrea told me.

"I know. I get that. It's hard to see someone else in pain. I do appreciate a person approaching me. I know they're being kind and it's better than walking past me without saying anything at all."

I paused.

"The part that's not so comforting is learning to accept that this hurt doesn't just go away."

I paused again, struggling to explain.

"Andrea . . . are you still there?"

"I'm here. I wish *I* had something to say," she replied.

"Listening is really the best thing you can do."

Her call moved me into my day with a new sense of interest. Even with the contradictions and tensions—loving my kids but being stung by their resemblance to Shawn; doubting God's purposes while clinging desperately to him; wanting to engage in life and quit life all at the same time— even though most of the signposts along this road didn't make sense, even though I was often filled with fear and insecurity, even in moving but not wanting to move, I decided the best thing was to move anyway.

To me, the concept of moving forward had always been linear. Now, the moving that I did within any given day was all over the map. My grief took many turns, had so many layers. Still, I was determined to keep my commitment to move, and that was productive. Despite all the switchbacks and hairpin curves, I was going somewhere—even if I couldn't yet name the destination.

When I got off the phone with Andrea my kids were in the fridge, seconds away from dripping maple syrup down the inside of the door.

"Mom, you see me?" Maddi giggled, "No, Mom! Don't see me, Mom!"

"Yes, I see you, Miss Maddi," I said. "And syrup isn't a beverage. Let's make some waffles for breakfast."

"Waffles!" Maddi cheered.

"Mom, can we poke our fingers in the middle and make big holes for glasses for our eyes?" Jordan asked.

"That's possible," I said and opened the freezer to find a box of waffles. *Find something to work on, think about, or do*, I thought.

"So, what should we do today?" I asked.

"Go swimming!" Jordan said.

"No, gim-nastics!" Maddi said in a huff to her brother. By nature, she liked to take charge.

"We could go to open gym at Flyaways Gymnastics today," I told them.

Two little pairs of eyes looked at each other, smiles peeping into grins, then looked at me and back to each other. I loved to see them excited, a refreshing change from the frequent moments of sibling rivalry.

Many days, I coaxed myself to watch my kids, even when I had no interest in playing with them, cooking for them, or teaching them. Just *be*.

It was a form of moving. Instead of getting upset with myself for not feeling "happy," I gave myself permission to just *be*—whatever that spectrum of shapes and patterns and topics looked like.

And that's what I did. Morning after morning. Hour after hour. Minute after minute. Whether it was emptying the dishwasher, turning on dance music for the kids and me, or sitting on my couch with only enough energy to thumb through a magazine, I was carried by the notion that my body and spirit could still move.

Even though my life connection with Shawn had died, I was still very much alive. Moving helped me to discover new perspectives on life and how to re-enter it. As I continued to journal and share some of my entries online, I began receiving e-mails from both friends and strangers asking me if I would consider writing a book.

As with grief, I became a student again. This time studying the world of writing. As I focused my energy in learning a new discipline, I could see glimpses of hope. Interest was returning to my spirit. Something had grabbed my attention and I could put my creativity there.

Slowly I worked to incorporate the loss of Shawn into my life without him. The concept reminds me of the lessons Shawn and I learned during our two years in the Peace Corps, living in Concepción de Maria, a small village in Honduras. We worked to adjust to a new culture, a new language, and a new way of life.

Those years transformed us. We were pushed to try new things and improve our talents. We became more patient with the villagers' sense of time, we adopted a simpler lifestyle, and we found new value in our relationship. Without a doubt, this experience provided us with a strong foundation for our marriage. The training we received while living in a developing nation inevitably developed us.

Sometimes we joked that, by our own multiplication, our time overseas added ten years to our marriage because of all the extra concentrated time we had together. If we were upset with one another, we had to work it out. There was only one door to our tiny living quarters, and it led straight up a stony mountain path. Shawn said we figured out quickly how to make things work between us so we wouldn't have to climb to the peak as an escape. After he died, I treasured the extra "ten years" we had—the high points and low points.

When we returned home to Minnesota, we naturally incorporated our Honduras experiences into life back in the States. We now spoke

Spanish fluently. We enjoyed mangos, black beans, and avocados. I had learned a guacamole recipe from the natives that I now shared with friends and family at parties and holiday get-togethers. No one questioned why I would want to adopt guacamole into my Midwestern palette. And our firsthand encounter with some of the many people in our world who live without access to clean and running water made Shawn and I appreciate the abundance we enjoyed in the United States. We began contributing to clean-water projects in Honduras and worked on fundraisers to raise awareness and aid. Our experiences influenced us to make a change.

After our service, no one asked if we were able to "let go" of that part of our life. The concept of "moving on" from our formative days in Honduras would have seemed absurd. That period in our lives would always be a part of us, affect us in some way, and add to who we were becoming. The Honduran days were a significant stretch of road in our lifelong journey, teaching us to take the good or the bad and do something with it.

Why would a relationship be any different? My life with Shawn would forever influence who I was and how I chose to continue living. With two young children asking me questions about their father, I needed to find a healthy way to incorporate and embrace our story of loss.

In taking the best I learned from Shawn and passing it on to our children, I found I could better cope with his death. Maybe this was a way for me to honor and remember his legacy. Perhaps even more profound, it is a way for me to honor and develop who I am to become.

Still, the grieving process requires balance. There are times when "let go" or "move on" have validity. In my own walk it's been important for me to let go of past regrets, obstacles, negativity, and a constant striving for perfection. I've also had to let go of control and the idea that I have a right to a certain life that I envisioned for myself.

Some people who've experienced loss get stuck in life. Their loss dominates to the point that their own lives become stagnant. I met one couple at a national memorial event in Washington, D.C., who became so consumed with attending memorial events for a relative—a fallen police officer—that they didn't have time to attend their own child's soccer games.

There's a time to remember and there is a time to release, a time to honor and a time to live.

I was alone one chilly Saturday afternoon, my kids were with their Uncle Mark and I was cleaning. "Brown Eyed Girl" came on the radio, and I started to dance. No one was watching, my dance was uninhibited.

The song ended and I slumped on a barstool at the kitchen island. I glanced at the calendar. *Four months. Seventeen days. That is how long it took to dance.* Was this part of finding a new life? I wondered how many more days I had to go before I got there.

Several months later, spring arrived and I opened all the windows to my house. Stagnant air was replaced with a light cleansing breeze. For a minute I soaked in the joy that comes with the return of warmth and sunshine.

Then panic came. I was tempted to close the windows. I didn't want to enter this new season without Shawn. The lighter air, the warmth through the glass pane, the melting snow—it conflicted with my hibernation of grieving.

How could I enjoy anything without Shawn? It didn't feel right. I didn't want to grieve forever, but I didn't want to be happy without him. In spite of my jumbled feelings, I forced myself to push through the anxiety. I left the windows open. I gave myself permission to feel good again, if even for a small moment. I was exercising my ability to engage.

Lack of movement immobilizes, I thought. *Engagement connects.*

Joy and sorrow can, indeed, coexist. And if we allow it, loss has the power to bring us into that sacred space of perceiving things in a new way, of teaching us what matters, of leading us to the height of living and to the depth of who we are—deeper than we have known before.

The act of moving within my hopelessness caused me to examine my faith and cling tightly to God's sustaining grace, which was a constant source of restoration and healing for me. Even without seeing him, I knew God was close. If I were to survive the multiple levels of doubt shaped by death, I needed to hang on to the hope of God.

Each time I engaged in writing as my method of *moving*, I was challenged not only to reflect on my beliefs but to decide which beliefs I would hold onto with confidence and passion. Staying stuck in depression, in self-doubt, or in denial of the life around me only prohibited me from mending the brokenness in my life. One can't restore something that is dead. Only God is in the business of resurrection. But, someone who is moving and trying and searching will reestablish their life and find renewal. This is God's grace at work in us.

One counselor told me the Mesopotamian legend of a woman stranded and left for desolate. Inanna had lost everything in her life including her own skin, bones, and blood. Walking through the forest one day with her Creator he told her, "Choose which parts you want back. Take the sinews and tendons and ligaments and make yourself new. Choose who you will be. Piece yourself back together one layer at a time. Choose carefully. Each layer has meaning. Be certain."

My daily commitment to move helped me to hope, to trust that there was something more. The more I would write, the more I could see possibility in my life. I began to expect life to return. I anticipated how my writing may one day help someone else and I connected this anticipation with hopefulness—a sense of worth to my writing and overall purpose for my living.

I trusted that God's plan for my life was bigger than my own. Like prayer, moving became my daily offering. By focusing on words such as *try, continue,* and *walk*, I would ask God to help me move throughout my day. I relied on God fully and, wounded though I was, experienced him holding me. I let him move me in his way—move his way in me, especially when I could barely move myself.

Still, on many days I pictured my future as a hopeless scenario. I was getting used to the roller-coaster groove of life and learning to live inside disappointment. I sometimes couldn't imagine where I would again find steady joy. If Shawn's death would always create in me a sense of regret, how could I find a desirable future without him?

I hated hearing that God would never give me more than I could handle. Or that I was so strong. I didn't want to be strong. I wanted to be my normal self living in my old-normal life.

The phrase, "God never gives us more than we can handle," isn't in the Bible. It is a misquoted idea taken from 1 Corinthians 10:13, which tells us that we will not be *tempted* beyond what we can bear and that if we are, God will provide a way out. In fact, 2 Corinthians 1:8–10 tells of the great pressure Paul felt, "far beyond our ability to endure."

There have been times when I have cried to God, "I can't do this anymore." It is in these moments when God climbs into my heartache with me. His strength takes over where my weakness has left off.

I scrawled a prayer in my journal on May 20, 2007:

> *God, when I am immobile, be my movement. You are*
> *my heart's healing. Take your place in me. You see*
> *all the dimensions that intersect grief. All the levels and*
> *layers of hurt. Be my promise for the future. Be my*
> *comfort for the past. Be my reflection for the moment.*
> *Take the plans you have ordained for my life, those which*
> *I cannot see, and help me to trust that they are good.*
> *Do not lose sight of me, for I am broken. Help me to be*
> *open to the new life that moves inside of me.*

I had the impression that God wasn't as concerned that I move forward as that I move with him. He loved me where I was. And he wanted me to experience his love by allowing him to move me toward healing.

Throughout the Bible God continually calls us to bring our burdens to him because he cares (Matthew 11:28–29 and 1 Peter 5:7). God heals the broken hearted and binds up their wounds (Psalm 147:3). He will be our Comforter in sorrow when our heart is faint (Jeremiah 8:18). If we place our trust and hope in him he will renew our strength (Isaiah 40:31). God invites us to ask for mercy and grace to help us in our time of need (Hebrews 4:16). God does not want to see us hurt. He wants us to heal. This is a sign of his great love for us.

God's grace was all I had—and all I needed. In the midst of Paul's great pressure, beyond his ability to endure, he still determined to set his hope on God, "that he will continue to deliver us" (2 Corinthians 1:10). In Paul's weakness, God said to him, "My grace is sufficient for you, for my power is made perfect in weakness" (2 Corinthians 12:9). God's message for me was clear: *Grace is sufficient. Trusting is sufficient. Moving is sufficient.*

I didn't know it at the time, but by simply moving and letting Christ take over, even though I felt weaker, I was becoming stronger. This was Christ's strength in me, definitely something outside my own capabilities.

God, show me. If your plan is small, move me toward acceptance. If your plan is big, move me toward courage. Help me to believe I am exactly where you have planned me to be. Help me to move. One last thing— help me to believe in something.

CHAPTER 8

Be Changed

We can kill the love so that it stops hurting. But, then of course part of us dies, too. Or, we can ask God to open up another route for that love to travel.

—CORRIE TEN BOOM

One night after bath time and before the litany of events that preceded bedtime, I surprised my kids with new matching pajamas. Jordan jumped out of the tub squealing, "Thank you, Mom! Congratulations!"

I laughed, "Yes, congratulations! You two will be twins."

Clapping his hands he added, "Congratulations, Mom! We're going to make you a Congratulations Heart!"

Madelynn expressed her own thanks with sparkly eyes and a big hug.

Jordan's exuberance caught me off guard. I noticed I was genuinely smiling. No trace of loss or sadness. I felt at ease—a sense of satisfaction. I was engulfed in the moment and the sweetness of my children. With such a show of enthusiasm, I felt a shower of much-needed appreciation.

Since Shawn died, I'd struggled with thankfulness—with finding things to be thankful for, with expressing thankfulness. My life was actually full of blessing yet, at the same time, stripped of blessing. Jordan's energetic response over new pajamas helped me to see the miracle in gratitude.

Far removed from the place I'd once been, I am now . . . different . . . from who I once was. The road to restoration involved not an actual restoration—that was not possible—but a rebuilding of every part of me like the story of the woman in the forest. Acknowledging gratitude for what I still had in my life was an initial piece of the project.

Reading through another old journal entry from our time in Honduras, I found a reference to the letter from Paul to the Philippians, which states, "Have no anxiety about anything, but in everything by prayer and supplication with thanksgiving let your requests be made known to God" (Philippians 4:6 RSV):

> *This is a good verse for me to remember. I may get anxious at times with everything around me. But if I truly look at my situation, there is much for me to be thankful for, like the fun trip and experiencing this whole thing together. As we document our time in Honduras, I'm finding that I love to write! This is another thing to be thankful for. One of my favorite pastimes is writing home. Maybe Shawn and I can write a book someday.*

Little did I know then how much I'd need my own advice to be thankful.

After my kids were in bed, I needed to talk to someone.

I found Deanna home, and as we talked she shared what she'd learned at church that morning. "The priest encouraged us to be thankful for what we have instead of dwelling on our deficits—what we don't have."

"The 'Abundance Theory,'" I replied.

"Yeah . . . there's enough to go around . . . enough to share."

"It's the opposite of the 'Scarcity Mentality,'" I said, "which hordes things—worried about running out."

"Exactly," she said.

"That's my challenge right there," I told my sister. "How do I find abundance when I feel so incomplete? Why would God bless me with Shawn only to take him away? It's hard to live with gratitude sometimes . . . many times. But I guess I should be happy that God has more in store."

I let out a sigh.

"You don't sound convinced," she said.

"I am, and . . . I'm not. I want to believe there's good in life, yet I'm a skeptic."

I was near tears and felt unsteady as I paced around the room. This was the too-familiar exhaustion of grief. I was tired of trying to figure out all the contradictions.

"I want to believe," I continued. "I want to believe in the idea of being in the right place at the right time. Shawn responded to his call that day. He likely saved someone else from getting killed—maybe a family of five driving farther down the road . . . another officer . . . the felon . . ."

I paused, and sat on the arm of the couch, "Do I do that, Dee? Am I living the life I was called to live?"

"Wow," Deanna said, more as a deep sigh of her own than an actual comment.

"I know," I said. "I think about these things too deeply. I just want to experience what God has for me in this life. But I'm confused. I'm so far from well with all of this . . ."

I couldn't finish. I told my sister I'd call her in the morning and hung up. My face, chin, and hands were wet from my tears. No . . . I was not well.

Before going to bed, I sat on the floor next to a heap of unfolded clothes in the corner of my room. I wanted to see hope. Not just snippets of hope when I found time to write. I wanted to see hope as a more constant. I concluded that if I was still alive, God must have a deliberate plan for me. If God was indeed good and if it was true that all good things come from him, I reasoned that I would need to identify and name the good things still evident in my life. I could see it as I might the pile of laundry next to me—either irritated about the mess, or thankful that I had clean towels. The Abundance Theory is all about perception.

See the beauty. See the blessing.

I began to feed these two phrases into my swirling thoughts as I attempted to recognize the beauty and blessing in my life. Those words became signposts for my healing.

I didn't deny I was hurting. But I knew I needed to do more than hurt. I needed to practice expressing my gratitude even if in small ways. Appreciation always broadens and deepens the view. It's easy to focus on the pain of loss because it's right in front of us. Still, it's healing to recognize something to be grateful for, which often comes in disguise. Just because the blessing isn't always obvious doesn't mean it isn't there.

Memories can provide some of our most abundant ground for gratitude. Certain smells or tastes take us back to distinct events or locations. For my first birthday without my spouse, my brother and sister bought me fresh lemon-grass tea, a flavor Shawn and I drank often in Honduras where the lemon-grass grew wild near our home.

One sip of the tea and I was taken back to the tight quarters of the two-room cement house, where we'd relax at night with the temperature never dropping below seventy-five degrees. I pictured the single, counter-top burner used to heat the water like a science experiment over a Bunsen burner. We squished the long, smooth, lemon grass stalks into the teapot to soak up the zesty flavor.

Shawn loved to make this tea in the evening and drink it while he wrote journal entries or e-mails to family and friends on our laptop.

"Jen, this is really living," he told me one night only weeks after we'd moved to the mountain village.

"Well . . . I don't like it," I replied.

"It'll get better," he told me.

"When?" I asked.

I was mad at myself. I felt like I hadn't fully thought through my romantic notion of an adventurous getaway. It had been my idea to travel, to move thousands of miles from home. It was my desire to learn more Spanish and try something bold. Living in a third world country among cockroaches the size of golf balls, and in temperatures well over a hundred degrees was solely my suggestion.

Shawn obliged mostly out of sheer devotion. He was definitely daring, but his idea of roughing it was short-term—camping for a week in the Boundary Waters of Northern Minnesota and then returning to civilization. Now he seemed to be doing much better than I was and we still had two years to go.

"Jen, we can only focus on what's in front of us. There's a reason we're here. And it's not all bad," he said.

"Not all bad? Shawn! We're living with spiders bigger than baseballs. Haven't you noticed? There're no grocery stores. No movie theaters. Nothing. We've given up good jobs—very good jobs—to live like this. I want to go home!"

My complaining only amplified my negative perspective. As I sat cross-legged on our double bed—the one piece of furniture we owned—Shawn kept typing. He knew that it was best to give me time to process until I calmed down.

A couple minutes later, I came out to the kitchen area where he was typing an e-mail to his brother. He got up to get more hot water.

"I'm sorry," I said. "I'm sorry I made you come here."

He turned around and sat me down in the chair next to him at the table (okay, we had two pieces of furniture).

"I'm not sorry, Jen. I like it here. I'm glad we came. And you will be too . . . eventually." A smirk appeared on his face. "After you forget about the scorpions in our shower and the roosters crowing at 4:00 AM."

"You're sure?" I asked. Filled with reservations, I nonetheless opted not to voice any more of my complaints.

"I like how quiet it is," he said. "I like the people here. I'm learning to like the food. And I like being with you. We have a lot to be thankful for." The smirk was gone, replaced with the confident look I knew well. He was determined to make this work.

I noticed his tea, the clean aroma permeating the room. Our neighbor, a local farmer, had cut it fresh from his field that morning and instructed Shawn how to use it. A gift given with no conditions.

Now, it had taken only one sip of my birthday tea and I could see Shawn again. The memory was strong, and I let it seep into me. I'd never realized that taste was related to memory, but now it was all connecting in my mind.

I could taste and see and smell the tea; the memory smooth and clean and calming. How good it is to appreciate a gift. I heard my husband's voice inside my mind, "We can only focus on what's in front of us . . . we have a lot to be thankful for." I let the memory teach as I prayed; *Help me see the blessing in front of me. Change me.*

The first time I took the garbage out by myself after Shawn died, I felt capable. It wasn't fun, but it wasn't horrible. It was cold. But I could do it.

I darted back into the house, thinking how thankful I was for every time Shawn had taken out the garbage. I'd never thanked him for this when he was alive. I never even thought about it. Now I realized how nice a gesture it was. How many things had Shawn done that I didn't notice or appreciate?

In a journal entry from Honduras, I wrote about a day we went hiking:

> *The hike was revitalizing. I plan to journey that*
> *way often. It did wonders for my state of mind and*
> *encouraged me to rely on the inner strength God provides*
> *when I feel I cannot possibly continue. I was reminded*
> *today that God doesn't place me in a situation without*
> *providing the strength I need to survive.*

I was telling my friend Chanttel during one of our three-hour lunches about the connections I was making between healing and thankfulness.

She listened, sitting forward in the restaurant booth and then asked, "Don't you feel strong?" It was more of a statement than a question.

"Yes," I said. *More than strong*, I thought, *I feel like a new person.*

"Doesn't it feel like you can do anything?" she asked.

I laughed out loud. I knew exactly what she meant.

"I do feel that way," I replied. "Like last week when I fixed my kitchen cabinet door. Home repair was never my territory or expertise. But the whole time I was working to figure it out I could imagine Shawn behind me saying, 'You can do this, Jen.'"

"Was it hard?" she asked.

"Well, it took me a few minutes to piece it all together. And I felt intimidated at first. But I just kept telling myself, 'You're brighter than any kitchen cabinet door!'"

"And?"

"I fixed it. And it made me feel strong," I told her.

"Because you *are* strong," she said. "We're stronger from what we've gone through. We *can* do this."

"I do see the benefit of trying," I told her. "But not everything goes together as well as the cabinet door."

"When you realize you're stronger than you think, then something's working," she said. "And that's something to be thankful for."

Oftentimes God writes other people into our stories to convey messages or provide comfort. My friends, Jeremy and Cindy, were one of the couples that I could be completely honest with, even when I felt my faith was floundering. One evening they visited for dinner and we discussed at length the idea of living in tension between blessings and battles.

"Each of us is whole," Cindy said. "We're just waiting for the character who is hiding to be unleashed, for the reality of who we are, the person God made us to be."

"Another way to put it," Jeremy said, "is *God sees us where we are and realizes our potential.*"

I marveled at that idea—of being broken and whole at the same time. Yet it accurately described my position.

In the Bible, the Beatitudes are an amazing reflection on blending wholeness with brokenness. God moves toward the brokenhearted. He works for the good of those who are hurting. From our Maker's perspective, there is value in brokenness. "Blessed are those who mourn, for they will be comforted" (Matthew 5:4).

Blessed are the broken, for God comes near our pain. He comforts us, often through the comforting that comes from others.

My parents were two of the most generous lifelines I had after Shawn died. They helped me around my house and with my kids, doing things I would forget to do like water my plants or put salt in the water-softener.

One day when my mom was at my house I told her, "I feel bad that I always have to call you to come over for something—either we're sick or haven't slept or I have an appointment. I feel like my disrupted life has completely rearranged yours."

She replied, "Jennifer, don't ever worry about calling me or your dad. I feel my best when I'm here with you and the kids."

"I still feel bad," I said. "It's hard to keep asking for help."

"I'll tell you this again," she said. "There's no place I'd rather be than with Jordan and Madelynn. Loving them is healing for me."

Considering my kids, I said, "Well, Jordan and Maddi definitely love their 'papa' and 'gamma.'"

"The feeling's mutual," my mom assured me.

But it's completely humbling to admit we aren't able to do it all on our own, that we need help. Among the numerous insecurities of loss, feelings of inadequacy add to our grief.

A month after Shawn died, a complete stranger showed up on my doorstep with a card.

Standing in my foyer, the young mom introduced herself and asked, "Is there anything I can do for you? Can I bring you food? Clean your toilets?"

I started crying, a bit embarrassed at my state, especially in front of someone I didn't even know. "On the weekends my family takes turns coming to my house, but Monday morning comes and I'm completely alone. I know they have work and life has to go on . . . but . . ."

I didn't know what else to say. How could I ask for help when I had no idea what I needed?

"Can I take your kids for you?" she asked.

I stared at her, my face blank. Would she really do that? I felt desperate. "Yes," I replied with pure relief and no further thought. I grabbed their jackets and shoes, nearly shoving my kids out the door.

She smiled, natural and unforced, a genuine expression that told me she was glad to help.

In less than five minutes, I realized what I'd done. I grabbed the phone and called Sergeant Bill at the police station. He'd become our family liaison whenever I needed to contact the department. To me, he was now family.

"Sergeant Bill! I just gave my kids to a total stranger!" I told him in a panic, hoping he didn't think I was completely unfit to care for my children.

In a voice forcing calm, he said, "You did what?"

"Well, she said she could help me and I didn't think it through and I'm so tired and can you do a background check?" I blurted in one breath and then gave him her name. "She said her husband is a police officer and she brought me a really nice card and letter."

"I'll call you right back," he said.

Minutes later the check was completed and Sergeant Bill called, "Your new friend comes back with rave reviews. You couldn't have sent your kids with a better person, Jennifer. It's okay."

"But, Sergeant Bill," I said, "I . . . I don't know her. She isn't my friend."

"She is now," he replied.

My new friend, Karissa, came to my home every Monday for a year to take my children and care for them along with hers. She chose to enter my world of despair and brought with her a nonjudgmental kindness. I learned the profound lesson that the gift of true friendship is the only thing next to God himself that got me through one moment to the next. She along with many others chose to be bold, uncomfortable, interested, and concerned. She chose to be changed.

God was, in fact, redefining my idea of generosity and how it works to fill us up and change us. Abundant giving matters. Healing takes root for both sides—the giver and the receiver.

One of the police officers Shawn had worked with, Officer Steve, came to our house one afternoon to help with a couple fix-it projects. He showed up at the door with a cordial grin, gave Jordan a high-five and waved at Maddi.

"Where's the light that isn't working?" he asked.

With a bit of pride in my voice, I defended myself in a roundabout way. "I'm learning how to do most of these things on my own. It's just the porch light is really high up. I think the bulb can only be changed with a ladder."

He seemed aware of the lack of self-confidence I was trying to hide.

"Don't worry about it, Jennifer, we want to help you. I grieve by fixing things. It makes me feel better. That's just me," he said with a shrug.

I'd recently learned that, in general, men grieve by working, doing, moving.

"Changing a light bulb is my therapy," he told me.

With the help of many, I thought, *I can do this.*

In the Beatitudes, God calls us not only to be comforted but to comfort those who are hurting. God blesses us out of our pain especially in the moment we show care for others. I knew I could comfort others who suffered loss, not because the situations would be identical, but because I could connect. In *The Root of Righteousness,* A. W. Tozer wrote, "It is doubtful whether God can bless a man greatly until He has hurt him deeply." We all can use our hurts to make a difference in someone else's life, and our own.

God uses giving to heal us. Giving fortifies our spirits. Second Corinthians 1:3–4 says, "God is our merciful Father and the source of all comfort. He comforts us in all our troubles so that we can comfort others. When they are troubled, we will be able to give them the same comfort God has given us" (NLT). The best sign of healing is when a griever is ready to help someone else.

An old Chinese tale in Harold Kushner's 1981 book *When Bad Things Happen to Good People* tells about a woman whose only son died and her search to drive sorrow out of her life:

> In her grief, she went to the holy man and said, "What prayers, what magical incantations do you have to bring my son back to life?" Instead of sending her away or reasoning with her, he said to her, "Fetch me a mustard seed from a home that has never known sorrow. We will use it to drive the sorrow out of your life."
>
> The woman set off at once in search of that magical mustard seed. She came first to a splendid

mansion, knocked at the door, and said, "I am looking for a home that has never known sorrow. Is this such a place? It is very important to me."

They told her, "You've certainly come to the wrong place," and began to describe all the tragic things that had recently befallen them. The woman said to herself, "Who is better able to help these poor unfortunate people than I, who have had misfortune of my own?" She stayed to comfort them, and then went on in her search for a home that had never known sorrow.

But wherever she turned, in hovels and in palaces, she found one tale after another of sadness and misfortune. Ultimately, she became so involved in ministering to other people's grief that she forgot about her quest for the magical mustard seed, never realizing that it had in fact driven the sorrow out of her life.

Giving is my mustard seed. When I take time to engage with my kids, giving them a part of my real self, devoting my time instead of thinking only of my sadness, I feel genuinely stronger. At church, when I sing with the band and later discover that someone had cried through an entire song because of the way it touched them, I feel the gracious connection of sharing a part of me with someone else who needed it.

One morning I read an e-mail from "Louise," a divorced mom raising two teenage boys. She told me that the previous night she was ready to give up. The way she described the situation implied she may have been contemplating suicide. A friend recommended that, before going to bed, Louise read my writings online. She could relate with what I wrote and thought, *If this Jennifer can keep going, so can I.*

The irony was that, the morning I received her e-mail, I felt overwhelmed by the day in front of me. I had little energy, let alone enthusiasm. But when I found I had encouraged her, I was moved. My experience had helped someone in a critical time. I had made a difference, and that was a strong statement when I was continually questioning if anything mattered without Shawn.

Extending a part of me widened my heart and broadened my view to encompass more than I could have ever seen before Shawn died. My giving opened up something inside of me, a place where what had been depleted could be filled. Giving told me that life was more than simply enduring; it could be strong.

My kids are my daily joy—and my daily work. Raising children isn't an easy task. I often feel lacking in creativity and patience. And sometimes I need to be reminded that my kids are a daily source of love.

One Saturday morning I woke up to a strange sound—silence. What were Jordan and Maddi doing? Usually they were at the side of my bed, chiding me to wake up, or running around the house chasing each other. I never needed to use an alarm clock. The unaccustomed quiet told me I should be prepared for a surprise.

As I trudged down the hallway connecting our kitchen and living room, I discovered my imaginative children playing in piles of oatmeal flakes, pretending it was snow. As they looked up at me with larger-than-life smiles, I spotted the brand new oatmeal container completely spilled out and abandoned in the corner. I stood stunned, not sure if I should scold or laugh or turn back for bed.

Jordan stared at me bravely and asked, "Mom, are you going to talk?"

I didn't say a word.

But Jordan couldn't stop talking. "Mom, are you going to talk to everything beautiful? Mom, are you going to talk to God? Mom, are you going to talk to Dad? Mom, are you going to talk to the birds and the plants? Mom, are you going to talk to me?"

Without a word, I scooped up my kids, carried them into the bathtub and started scrubbing matted oatmeal out of their hair. When they were bathed and halfway back to normal, I placed them on the couch, letting them chatter as I found the broom and began sweeping up mounds of oatmeal "snowflakes."

Then I noticed an unfamiliar sensation. Peace. A whisper inside me said, *You can handle this.* Just like Chanttel had told me, I was strong. I could handle this large, unexpected mess.

Jordan was still searching for a reply from me. "Mom, what should we do? Clean it up?"

Finally I spoke. "Yes . . . we can clean it up."

Madelynn started to sing, *"Clean up. Clean up,"* to the tune of a nursery rhyme. And helping each other, we worked to put the house back in order.

There is good, I thought, *and we will find it.* Gradually. In no set order. Moment by moment. And in between moments.

It was happening in small ways. Like my fixing something around the house or having lunch with a friend. One night while I was reading stories to my kids, I realized I was enjoying our time together. *How does that happen?* I asked myself. *How can I enjoy this?*

One answer: I could see the good that was still in my life, when I was thankful for the present moment and for the people within that moment. Gratitude is a fundamental instrument used to create change on our healing journey. Gratitude makes a way to say, *I can do this.*

Why do I need to write?

Many reasons. But near the top of my list is that I don't want to look back in future years and think, *I missed you, Jordan. . . . I don't remember our highlights, Maddi.* Grief absorbs everything like a sponge, and I don't want it to suck up my blessings, capturing the memory and awareness of them, like it sometimes does when I'm not making a conscious effort to write them down.

One of those times had occurred on a particularly cold winter evening about a year and a half after Shawn died. My sister Cynthia called to make plans for the weekend.

"Oh . . . hi," I said, my voice flat, unenthusiastic.

"What's going on over there?" she asked.

"I'm miserable. I'm so tired of feeling close to good only to have it disappear." I was slumped on the floor in front of the fireplace, letting my feet warm up before I went to bed.

I hated giving the same report over and over. How many times would I go over this with my sisters?

"Jen, remember . . . you need to list what you're thankful for," Cynthia told me.

"Nothing. I have nothing." I stared at the glass doors on the fireplace, wishing I could break them, but knowing it would just be one more thing in the house I'd need to fix.

"That isn't true," she said. "Tell me right now five things that you're grateful for."

"It's always the same list of things," I replied, disinterested.

"Okay, so what's the list?" she asked.

"Jordan Madelynn my health writing my family," I droned in one breath.

"That sounds like a lot to me . . . go write that down . . . Now." Her tone brooked no argument.

It was enough to snap me out of my self-pity. She was right. I'd flippantly listed the good things in my life—the *best* things in my life—as if they were leftover items at a garage sale. Writing held me accountable. Writing nudged me to appreciate what I still had in my life.

We don't need to be gifted writers, or even good writers. Anyone can write a list of five things for which they are thankful. And the truth is, I have—we all have—amazing blessings surrounding us every day.

The next weekend I was off to a writing retreat in Charlotte, North Carolina. I dropped my kids off at my mother-in-law's house, anxious about leaving—it was hard to balance life between kids and my therapy of writing. With tears I told her, "I don't know if I should be going. I hate leaving my kids. I don't feel like a very good mom."

Bonnie hugged me and told me, "Nonsense, you are a very good mom. Before you worry about writing, take a few minutes to sit in the sun and relax. Your kids need some grandma time . . . I need some grandma time. They will be fine." She knew that my love both for my children and for writing helped me find significance for living. Her permission to take care of myself was what I needed when I couldn't seem to give myself permission.

Three hours later I was on a shuttle bus to my hotel. The bus driver made small talk while I tried to read—"Where're you going . . . where're you from?"—but I was unwilling to be pulled out of myself.

Small talk. Small world, I thought. *I live in a small, short-term world.*

"Where's your family?" he continued with his twenty questions.

I put my book down. It was obvious I wouldn't be reading. "I came alone." The words sounded sad and lonely.

"Oh. That sounds like a nice break," he said.

"Actually, I'm here for a workshop," I told him.

Still thinking of his question about my family, I dwelled on Shawn's and my hope to have four children. If he were alive, would I have a family of six? Now our family consisted of three. I wanted to tell the driver that half my family was missing, but knew it was crazy to explain. I stared out the window. The driver was finally silent.

But now I was the one who wanted to talk. I took the risk and said out loud, "I'm going to find myself here. Writing helps me discover who I am."

"Then I'm glad you made the effort to come," he said, grinning, but didn't ask any more questions.

I walked into the hotel lobby, ready to meet myself. If I couldn't find the young woman I was looking for, maybe I was ready to re-create her.

At the conference's first writing session, the speaker talked about taking risks. He told us that in order to be good writers, we must be endangered by our writing—we must be willing to dig into our thoughts and feelings, express what they really are, be embarrassed, be exposed.

It seems like the same formula for processing grief. Grief forces me to be vulnerable. The only way through it is to dissect it, explore every depth and every experience that it has for me. I will risk being myself in my grief and in my writing in order to salvage the life inside of me.

Shawn and I believed that God had a calling for our lives together. I wondered what my calling was now.

I knew I had a desire to write. Writing helps me feel better. But I couldn't believe I was walking through grief just to learn how to deepen my writing. Shawn didn't die so I could become a writer. No, it was the reverse—writing supported me through his death.

There are many ways to find support through grief—many things that can help us to feel better about living. One woman who e-mailed me shared her love for scrapbooking. She designed photo books of her spouse for her young son. Her creativity became a profession and she now works out of her home designing layouts for a major scrapbook company. Another friend told me that she began volunteering with a local food shelf after her child died. She also found it rewarding to make anonymous donations to various charities in her daughter's name.

At a support group, I learned of a widower who joined a baseball league. The exercise helped him channel his anger and included the unexpected surprise of meeting new people—some of whom he now considers his closest friends. The list of possibilities is long, probably endless—a cooking club, gardening, working on cars, reading a book, planning a vacation. Ambitions can be big or small. Overall the idea is to find something engaging—something that will gently draw you like a magnet, attracting a change in mood and pulling you back to life.

The hard part about doing something we used to take pleasure in or attempting something new is that we may not feel like doing anything at all. Reaching out of our grief into a new life endangers us—we need to risk it anyway.

I remember talking to my aunt about fear. Her advice was, "Do it afraid."

There has been plenty to frighten me over the past couple years. Still, I find when I make an effort there is a source of delight that follows, even if it's small. The very thing we do that we enjoy could become much more than just a hobby or job. It may become our vocation.

My therapy is becoming my ministry. Writing is my support system to find my calling, my way to see a bigger God, working in a bigger picture, wanting me to walk closer with him.

Each of us, in our own way and on our own timeline, can find what supports us—what moves us can help us discover the persons we were created to be. We can believe in who we are becoming.

One thing is certain; we will be changed.

CHAPTER 9

Take the Time

There are not many things in life that take us through
so many emotions at the same time. This whole ordeal
has taken us from horror to shock, grief, sadness, joy and
happiness and then back to sadness again.

—GRAHAM MULLIGAN (AFTER THE RESCUE OF
THREE MINERS—TWO ALIVE, ONE DEAD)

Three months after Shawn died, a photo-lab tech called. "You have pictures to pick up at the store."

I was startled. "Are you sure?" I asked. "I don't remember bringing in any film."

"Yes, you had some photos developed on September sixth and you need to come pick them up," she replied.

I could hear her shuffling through a stack of envelopes and imagined I was only one on her long list of calls for the day. I wasn't sure what to say, so I did what I was becoming skilled at—I said nothing.

"Ma'am, are you there?" the technician asked, her voice curt.

"Oh . . . yes," I said, "I'm still here."

"Well, your photos have been in the old bin for some time now."

"Okay." I was immersed in thought. *What's the date anyway? Isn't it still September? I always pick up my photos on time.* My mind flipped through a mental calendar until it reached December. Three months past due. *When had December come?* I tried to concentrate on what she was telling me.

"If you don't come in by the end of this week, we'll have to throw the photos away," she said. "We don't have enough storage for all the old photos."

"Uhmm . . ." I started, my voice barely audible. "My husband died on September sixth. That's why I haven't picked them up. I didn't even remember that's what I did the morning he died."

"Well, I'm sorry about that. Do you want me to save the photos until Friday?" Her voice was brief and brisk, just like her method of sorting envelopes, which I could still hear in the background.

"Yes," I said.

She hung up. I glanced down at the receiver in my hand, dumb-founded once again by the effects of grief.

"Oh, by the way," I said, even though she was no longer on the line, "do you sell time at your store? Because I'm interested in buying a few months. Maybe you can call me with a reminder when time goes on sale."

The lab tech wouldn't have entertained my nonsense. Anyway, she had other calls to make. She wouldn't have been able to relate to my time warp. In fact, neither could I.

Shawn's death had drastically altered my arranging of time. Our days used to have transition—time when we were together, time for Shawn to go to work, family time. We scheduled our plans around him, and I used to say things like, "We'll eat when Daddy gets home," or "We'll go hiking on Dad's day off," or "Let me check Shawn's schedule and I'll call you back."

Time used to have segments. Now the days slurred together, followed by the smearing of weeks. How was it possible to lose an entire month, let alone three? How did I suddenly lack the sense to distinguish time? I wanted to call the photo lab back and yell at whoever was unlucky enough to answer, "Someone give me time back!"

Because I no longer had a reason to, I no longer felt like making new plans. Events happened. I attended. I followed other people's invitations. But living inside other people's calendars was not where I wanted to be. I wanted to track my own time again. And I wanted that time to include Shawn. I wanted to plan *our* summer vacation, schedule a date for *us*, and have a need to check *our* calendar. Instead my days consisted of living moment to moment minus any type of strategy.

One night I cried out to God, *When do I get to have an agenda again? When do I get to make a plan that outlives this week? Or even have the interest? I want my life back!*

In the middle of my tantrum, my spirit sensed God's message clearly. *You are living the exact way I intend you to live. This moment is exactly where I want you to be. I don't want you continually to rehash your past. I don't want you to focus or fret about the future. I want you in the here and now. I don't want you to return to how you were living. Instead of trying to find what others have, share with them what you have found. Living in the moment will change your life.*

I called Andrea the next morning to tell her what had happened with the photos.

"I need to work on something. I'm consumed with this idea that keeps surrounding me—to stop obsessing over time, to live now," I told her.

"I'm sure you are," she replied. "It's a powerful message."

"I don't want to miss time, like what happened with the pictures."

"Jennifer, that happens to people even when someone in their life hasn't died," she said.

"I know," I replied. "I'm just overwhelmed by how sad I feel. I'm so sad he's gone. I loved spending all my time with him."

"I know," she said.

"One thing I'm learning . . . there's no timeline to grief. I don't think *time* will heal me. I think that's God's job."

"Jen, you are entitled to take all the time you need," my friend told me.

"It's hard when I hear people tell me that time heals all wounds. What if this wound is too big?" I asked.

"It's not too big for God," she assured. "Tell me what you need. What can I help you with?"

"Well, it's almost Thanksgiving and I want to give something meaningful to both sides of my family."

"Okay, I'm on it . . . What about that cross Dana gave you?"

"Yes, the 'clinging cross,'" I agreed.

"I'll call her," Andrea said, "she'll know exactly how to help us."

I'd worked with Dana for over three years when I started my career in human resources. At the time she was my supervisor. Now she was my mentor and a great gift giver. Only weeks after Shawn died she'd given me a cross made of olive wood. The artist, Jane Davis, wanted to design something tangible to hold onto during times of crisis—reminding herself and others of God's ever-presence.

One constant through my grief walk—God was present. Even with all my changing emotions, God did not change. Whether I acknowledged him or not, he was there. And in spite of my battle with time, God remained.

I couldn't hide from the discoveries I was making—about myself, my children, my perceptions of reality. I was immersed in life at full-strength. Broken open. Shells crumbling. Barriers dissolving. Time erupting. My only healing option was to cling to God.

Still, I was distracted, wrestling with yet another dichotomy—I was oblivious to and simultaneously obsessed with time. Each day that was added to the grieving process multiplied my anxiety: I didn't want to keep marking time, saying, "It's been a month . . . it's been six months . . . it's been a year." Neither did I want to reach a point where the milestones no longer mattered, when I could admit, "I've accepted this." I didn't want acceptance to erase my former life.

Denial is a much safer place than acceptance. I could stay closer to Shawn there. Time carries me farther away from all my moments with Shawn. Like vision going blurry, my mind has increasing difficulty recalling his physical features, his face, his voice, his expressions. I see his smile in the photograph on our piano, and I can't remember him the way I used to. The smile is frozen in time with great warmth and yet I can't conjure up the last time I saw him with that smile. I want to take another snapshot and memorize a day with him.

It made me anxious that my recollections of Shawn's face were becoming like my recollections of what I had for dinner last Wednesday.

Why do memories start to fog and blur? The passage of time is like a walking belt at the airport. Once we step on, there's only one way to go. The passage of time isolates us from the past.

It was isolating me.

After Shawn died, I found myself meticulously organizing my house. It became a daily goal to thoroughly clean out a different closet, corner, or crevice. Some might look at my pursuit to make my house tidy as striving to bring order out of chaos, but it was more of an effort to ready myself. Paranoia followed me around my home. The next time tragedy knocked at my door, I'd be prepared for the shocking news. Everything would be in place.

The idea of preparing for tragedy is not only unreasonable, it's impossible. Still, I folded my laundry promptly so in case of bad news I'd have time to cry incessantly. My dishes would be done so I could have time to concentrate on all the new changes that were guaranteed to follow. The bins in the closets would be labeled so I didn't have to waste time looking for something that a new friend might need. I bought enough toilet paper to last a year, and my pantry was full of food so I wouldn't have to shop, taking time away from dealing with any new catastrophe.

Telephone numbers would be alphabetized to streamline making emergency calls. I would not let disaster stun me again, would not allow pandemonium to stagger me: "Okay. Now I have time to deal with you." I vowed, *Shawn, the next time they come to tell me that you died, I am going to be ready.* I didn't want to relive the type of turmoil that engulfed me when I first received the knock on the door. The thought was irrational: *If I make my house perfect, the effects of grief won't crush me so badly next time. I won't be existing in a blur, losing months out of my life.* I didn't want to be wounded like that again.

My wound was healing from the outside in. It was like a physical injury, red and raw, throbbing. The agony made me immobile and forced me into survival mode—unable to schedule, organize, observe the passage of time like I did before.

We can see how time affects a physical wound, working to heal the outer layer first, covering it with new tissue, new skin, and new life. Over time the wound scars, a testimony to the trauma—a reminder of how the body was hurt. Beneath the body is still healing and if pushed too fast there is a risk of reopening the wound only to add further complications and possible damage.

Time influences emotional and spiritual wounds too, contributing to the healing process layer by layer, day by day, from outside in. But the effects aren't as easy to detect. On the outside I appeared to be operating sufficiently. I could take care of my house. I could take my kids to swimming lessons. I could even pay my bills (although often late). The outside can be deceiving. The inside was still recovering.

Healing was something I didn't want to rush just so others would be impressed by my progress. As the oldest in my family, I've always been a pleaser, working hard at doing things "right," believing that was the way to gain approval and acceptance from my parents, teachers, and siblings. In friendships I often wouldn't express my true opinions, fearing that people would find them silly or of little importance. Others may have seen me as shy, quiet, or sensitive, but these qualities were all products of my larger insecurities—that people wouldn't like my true self.

Healing from the wound of loss, though, is too important to surrender to my insecurities. I needed to know that my healing was authentic, and not something that would later haunt me because I didn't take the time initially to address each part. If I were pushed into healing, the wound was at risk of reopening.

To be real and lasting, healing cannot be hurried. We need to take the time that it takes. Period. God knows how to heal us, and God's work is not dependent on time. Even if on the outside we appear better, we can still hurt on the inside. If we push too quickly for whatever reason—to meet the approval of others, to "get on" with life, to avoid what we perceive as obsessing—we threaten the work that God has begun in us.

Outside in. One thing I know. I need to trust God.

Yet another contradiction. I trust God, but at the same time I search. I wanted to know when I would finally be well again. An e-mail I received said that it takes one thousand days to grieve the loss of a loved one. Almost three years. A book I read suggested that total adjustment to a new life is about a five-year process.

My studies pointed to the idea that great loss takes great time to work through. I read Psalm 23 over and over, noticing the details of each word as a guide for grieving. The word that continues to come through to me is *walk*. "Even though I *walk* through the valley of the shadow of death . . ." Here, I find a reference to the pace of grief.

I need to walk through the valley of my loss. Walk. Not run. Not run away. The pace set by King David in Psalm 23 is patient and enduring. God *walks* with me.

Does time heal, as many people advised? My reality is that time lessens the initial intensity of pain. Time softens and time helps. Time makes a difference. Time is part of the design in the healing process. It is not the cure. Pain lessened is not pain eliminated.

Ultimately, God heals. Ecclesiastes 3:1 says, "There is a time for everything," and only God knows that timeline. This explains how it's possible for different people to have different measurements and methods for healing. God places time in our lives and uses it as a tool to heal us. But the tool is not the trainer. God is the master behind the healing.

One night I washed a bag of Shawn's T-shirts, which had been bunched up into a plastic bag and pushed into the corner of my bedroom for over two years. They were the last shirts he wore the week before he died. In the days following his death, I refused to wash them, wanting his scent to linger for as long as possible. As time passed I couldn't find the will to wash them. They served as some form of preservation. Not that dirty shirts could ever replace Shawn, but the mind does funny things after loss.

Two years later, I reevaluated the situation. The scent had disappeared, replaced by a collection of dust. It was time to wash them.

As I threw the clothes into the washer, a sensation came over me. The action of washing his laundry connected me to the time when I lived as his wife, and for a half a second I forgot he was dead. I was filled with the illusion that he may, indeed, need to wear the shirts that week, and that it was a good thing I was finally getting around to doing laundry.

Shaking my head at the absurdity that trails grief like a stray cat, I wasn't sure what I would do with the shirts once they were clean. But sometimes it's best to start a project and let it work itself out.

The shirt incident reinforced that grief does not follow a certain timeline. Some people might have washed the shirts immediately to give away; others may have never washed them at all. As I listened to the shirts spinning in my washer, I thought about how grief also twists and turns, attacking from various angles at unpredictable moments and from unpredictable directions. I thought most of all about how death is permanent. Shawn would never come back to wear the clothes I was washing.

Trying to ignore my thoughts over a bag of shirts, I threw them into the dryer and went upstairs to bundle up my kids and put them in the car. We were going to Karissa's house. She'd offered to watch them for me that morning so I could get some writing done. When we got there, I slumped onto her living room floor.

One look at me and she asked, "What's wrong?"

"Karissa, I feel this quiet chaos choking me. Where's God?"

She replied, "It's possible to be in the will of God even when everything seems to be in commotion."

"Most of the people I see don't seem to get what's important. I have a hard time relating to them," I told her. "We live in such a temporary world, but act like we'll be here forever."

My friend nodded.

"We want to control the uncontrollable. The way we spend money, decorate our homes, take pictures, fill our closets with thingamajigs called treasures—half the time forgetting what we bought. What for? It all disappears!"

She kept listening.

"Shawn didn't take anything with him," I said. "Not his work boots, not his palm pilot, not his beloved camera. Nothing. Why do we place importance on things that don't matter?"

I didn't know if I really wanted her to answer. She just let me keep going.

"Life's full of contradictions. Take materialism for example. We're not supposed to be wrapped up in material items, yet we're surrounded, consumed, and devoured by things."

Karissa was now sitting on her knees. "I know, it's so much," she said.

"We live like we'll never die. But then one day someone you really love dies, and then how're you supposed to live?" I was tired of thinking about this so much.

"Do you feel like writing?" she asked.

"Maybe," I said.

"Leave your kids here for as long as you like. Go home, shower, write—drink coffee. Jennifer, you need to do something for *you*," she told me.

"Okay," I said looking down, more like a murmur. "Thank you."

I went home and did exactly what she advised. I brewed a dark roast of chocolate flavored coffee and jumped into the shower.

With the hot water running over me, I thought about what used to consume my time: weekend plans, cooking, enjoying our photo hobby, creating to-do lists for both Shawn and me. Life wasn't like that for me anymore. Life felt extreme and short.

Drying off, I slipped into comfortable sweats and a long-sleeved T-shirt. I spent my morning with my journal and coffee:

> *God, balance me. How can I balance life within heaven's*
> *conception? How can I keep perspective? How can*
> *I contribute to life while setting my heart toward an*
> *eternal treasure? Can earth and heaven work together?*
> *Lord, open my eyes to see what matters. Fix my eyes on*
> *now. Today is just a shadow of tomorrow when we*
> *will soon be with you. You, O God, are forever.*

I am no longer comfortable in a world governed by time. Something inside of me remains unsettled and unsatisfied. I can see the temporariness of life by simply examining how those around me—including me—fill time: on the phone, returning e-mails; looking for new clothes, detesting old clothes; getting haircuts, degrees, new pets; rushing through holidays, climbing up ladders for careers, climbing down ladders for family, muddling through household chores—on goes the list of our striving for more in a world where nothing lasts.

As long as the list can get, only the moment directly in front of us is guaranteed. Still, we buy things for our houses or worry about something that has offended us as if we'll live forever, and as if collections of things and worries are all part of a long-lasting package.

There's a myth in American culture that says: more things, nicer things, make us happier. Traveling taught me differently. I've visited some of the poorest nations of Latin America and found truer joy in people who have nothing than in some of my wealthiest friends in the United States who are floundering for contentment.

So where is lasting contentment found? Why did God create us to live on an earth that won't last? When our hearts are conflicted and we desire to ease the mystery, we need to concentrate on what we know to be lasting.

God created us to know him, love him, and serve him—forever. God created us to one day be in heaven with him. God made us for eternity, and eternity is written on our hearts. God did not create people for a temporary purpose. That's why my heart was held captive by the loss of my spouse; I'd wanted our relationship to be long-lasting—permanent.

There's no debating that when we have something good in our lives we want it to continue. That longing is natural. But only heaven is permanent. Only in heaven will our cravings be satisfied, hurts become fully healed, and our longings made complete.

Death, then, is not only a part of life but the point of life. Death is the stepping stone from all we are and have and do on this earth, to our perfection in God's eternal presence. That preparation for eternity will take my lifetime. Why hurry it—or hold back? God's healing is preparing me for the permanency of heaven, not my temporary wishes on earth.

My questions changed from, *When will I get better?* to *How will God work inside my heart today?* Answering my own question requires daily examination. I don't do all that well at it. Even knowing that God is at work, I still want Shawn back so God can work in us together. The lonely route without him never looks appealing.

Yet how can I best honor the time I have left in my life? Am I using my passions or floundering in self-pity? Instead of worrying about the time it takes to heal, I strive to walk with my hurts and my passions, accepting that they both compose who I am.

I am passionately aware that, each day, I am living within temporary time. I ask myself, *What did I do today that mattered?*

One night when Shawn was still alive, when we were lying in bed rehashing our day, he told me, "I'm thankful for the way we live."

"What do you mean?" I asked.

"I have no regrets," he said.

"Well . . . that sounds like a good thing," I replied.

"I like knowing that when I lay my head on the pillow at night I'm not filled with guilt about things I'd like to do over," he said.

"Like what?" I asked.

"Like in my job, I see it all the time . . . police officers see people who have lots of remorse. People stuck and sorry—paying for their actions. I'm glad I don't have to worry about all the stuff I encounter—all the stuff people battle."

"You're good at leaving work at work," I said.

"It's more than that," he said. "Everything we do has consequences. If I can teach our kids anything, it will be that. All choices have consequences—good or bad. It's all about what we choose."

I laid my head on his chest.

"I want my conscience clear so I can sleep at night," he concluded.

As I reflect on his idea of consequences, I contemplate my current situation. Am I living with regrets? Am I stuck in the effects of my choices, and sorry? What am I choosing? Do I contribute to something of value each day?

Here is the definite: What ultimately matters is how I spend the time I have been given—how I serve, how I love, how I live.

Our society tends to ignore death. We don't talk about it and we don't know what to do with it when it arrives, even though it's a common denominator in all of our lives. Death scares a lot of people, and they're hushed and timid about the subject. The truth is, we don't like limits, and we don't like to think about our limited time. An even greater truth is that our life legacy is connected to how we've spent the time we have been given.

During a memorial event at the state capitol grounds—a candle-lighting ceremony in memory of all fallen officers—I was asked to speak at the service.

I shared memories about Shawn—how he loved gadgets, how he could whistle in tune. And I asked those in the audience to share memories of their loved one with someone who would listen. It feels good to share our stories and say the name of the one who died out loud. This exercise brings validity to how they touched our lives. One counselor advised me, "Talk about Shawn. Talk about Shawn. And talk about Shawn some more. Talk about him to whoever will listen. Talk about him until you can't think of anything else to say."

I concluded my talk with the idea that the Law Enforcement Memorial is not a tribute to the dead, but really an encouragement to the living. The legacy of those we love can inspire us to spend our time well. It can help us ask, "What kind of legacy will I leave? How do I want to invest my time?"

Shawn was my inspiration to live well. The way he invested his time, the way he lived, moved me. I witnessed how his life had helped change the lives of many others for good. I want to do the same. God has given me talents to write and speak and a heart of compassion. I want to invest my time, using my gifts.

Shawn knew that to use time well took planning. I wanted to set the clocks five minutes fast to get to places on time, but he was very punctual and didn't like that game.

"The problem isn't the clock," he would tell me.

He coached me on how to be someplace on time: factor the time needed to get ready, include the time to get the car loaded, and add time to make a quick stop at the gas station. "You can't just leave the house at the same time you're meant to be somewhere," he'd tease.

Shawn seemed to respect time, spending it wisely. He bought a book about sprinkler systems and designed one for our new yard. His friend John helped him install it and then helped him again when Shawn decided to lay sod for the yard. These projects all took time, but they saved money—to Shawn a good trade-off.

Shawn did many of our home improvements on his own, and I often wondered why it was hard for him to ask for help. When it came time for him to Sheetrock our unfinished basement, I was the one who called my dad and brother, Adam, to help, and then ask both of our moms to help paint.

Shawn respected others' time. One day I asked him, "Why don't you call Mark to help you with some of these projects?"

"Oh, I will," he said. "But I don't want to bother him with minor things that I can do. He knows how to do some of the finer details that I'll need help with."

Mark worked in construction before his job as an engineer, and Shawn looked up to his older brother in many ways. Mark's praise of Shawn's work affirmed that Shawn had spent his time well and done a good job.

Though punctual and efficient, Shawn could also spend hours doing things he loved. He could lose hours working on the computer. And I would tease him that he was one of the only people I knew who liked to read manuals to figure out how something worked. Most people won't spend time on that. But he also loved to read books, especially about the multidimensional attributes of God, about how God isn't constrained by time.

Shawn seemed to have the gift of living in the now.

He was a good cook, experimenting with recipes and, unlike me, had patience for redundant tasks. One time I decided to make homemade caramel sauce for ice cream. I didn't read ahead on the recipe, and when I discovered it needed to be stirred constantly over low heat for *fifteen minutes*, I quickly lost interest. Shawn came into the kitchen right about the time I was considering abandoning my project. He took over and stood there, stirring until the caramel was smooth and creamy.

"How can you do that?" I asked.

"Do what?" he responded, calmly concentrating on the sauce.

"Stand there! I grow impatient so easily."

"I don't mind repetition," Shawn laughed. "Good thing you married me."

Indeed.

My character has been significantly sharpened.

Accepting myself in all my anxiety, my doubts, my despair, my small movements, was an initial step to acceptance—accepting that loss would be integrated into my life. The path to acceptance was orchestrated by God and his own timetable. A path that said, this is the real me.

In order to become the people we are meant to be, we need to take time to daily connect with God to discover the skills, talents, and knowledge that he is refining in us. We need to center ourselves in those things. Connection to God can come differently every day—in a passing prayer while driving in the car, humming a song on the radio, interacting with our kids, doing whatever we call moving.

We don't have to be perfect. We don't even have to be good enough. What we do in Christ will be enough—more than enough.

During our grief journey it's easy to compare our timeline for healing with someone else's. We don't need to compare our hurts, our successes, or our outcomes with the world around us or even the neighbors around the block. It takes constant reminding that what helps one person heal will not necessarily help you heal or help me heal. And what looks "normal" or like something to be envied from the outside can be deceiving. Every person's story carries intricacies unique to their own heart.

On my timeline through grief, I am learning to trust my own instincts about what is best for me, to listen to the contradictory truths that coexist inside of me, and to confidently trust God's healing power to work its way through me. He is slowly restoring my confidence.

On a muggy August night nearly a year after Shawn died, I couldn't fall asleep, and wrote in my bedside journal: "My life is about answering a call. One that I never imagined receiving, never intended to respond to, and never realized how life shaking, life interrupting, life changing it would be."

Late that night, looking up at the ceiling I asked, *God, when will I believe in something again?*

I heard a rustling in my spirit, *That takes time.*

I turned over on my side and stared out the window through the slits in the blinds. *I get that,* I replied, *but* when *do you restore beliefs?*

The last thing I remember before drifting off was a quiet murmur, *I'm working on that.*

CHAPTER 10

Choose Love

I believe that imagination is stronger than knowledge—
myth is more potent than history—dreams are more
powerful than facts—hope always triumphs over
experience—laughter is the cure for grief—love is
stronger than death.

—ROBERT FULGHUM

Two days after Shawn died, his partner, Mike, who witnessed the entire scene, came to visit me. Mike was one of the last people ever to see Shawn alive.

Maybe he could help me understand exactly what happened. Maybe he could answer the questions that pulled at my heart, desperate for a different outcome.

"It was just like in the training videos, Jennifer," Mike said. "Shawn did everything right. None of us expected that car to go off the road."

For an hour we rehashed the lines and stances and last three running strides of my husband's life. No matter how long we talked, though, Shawn's death would never make sense. We both wiped tears from our eyes.

"I have one thing to ask you," Mike said.

"Okay," I replied.

"The night before Shawn died, we were both working B-shift, and on our dinner break Shawn says to me, 'I have the best wife ever.'"

I couldn't help but smile. It felt like a message from my husband.

Mike kept talking, "Well . . . I looked at him and said, 'Oh, yeah? Why's that?' and he tells me, 'Hey, man, when I got home from work last night there was a note on the stairs from Jennifer telling me to wake her up. It was 4:00 AM.'"

I bit my lower lip, eager to hear more.

"Then Shawn told me, 'When I woke her up she gave me a half-hour neck massage until I fell asleep,' and he kept bragging, 'Yep, I have the best wife.'"

I could tell Mike was happy that something was making me smile.

"What I want to know is . . . was that true?"

"Yes . . . that's true. Shawn had to work late that night on computer stuff and I knew his neck would be tense—making it hard to sleep."

"Jennifer," Mike said, "that's love. That really is love."

That neck rub was my *cup of water* to Shawn in the middle of the night. And now in his death, that act of serving became a portion of comfort to me. It was a confirmation of genuine love in the midst of many doubts and questions.

Two nights before Shawn died, he served me in his own way. It was 1:00 AM and he'd just gotten home from second shift. Ignoring my need for sleep, I had waited up for him.

"Lucy, I'm home," he said, like Ricky Ricardo from the 1950s television reruns we watched as kids. Giving me a kiss on the cheek he commented, "You're still up?"

I smiled, but he didn't notice because he went straight to the bedroom to throw his watch and wallet on the dresser. Coming back out to the kitchen to boil water for maté, an Argentinean tea, he said, "I'm going downstairs to do a couple things on the computer and pay the electricity bill."

"Oh . . . so you don't want to spend any time with me?" I asked, clearly feeling sorry for myself.

"Jen, that's nonsense. Get some sleep. I'll be up in an hour," he told me.

"Shawn, I waited up for you."

"Thank you, that was nice. I promise I won't be long," he replied, leaning toward me.

I dodged his second kiss and in a huff turned toward our bedroom without saying a word.

"Jen, don't be like that," he called out and hurried downstairs, no longer as eager to accommodate my mood.

I crawled into bed, muttering. Within five minutes, Shawn came upstairs and eased into bed beside me. I acted like I was already asleep. He wrapped his arms around me and snuggled close, whispering right above my ear. "Jennifer, *you* are my priority. And I don't want you up here wondering if you are. I've told you this before; my main goal in life is to make you happy."

I couldn't help but smile and replied, "Tell me again."

"Oh, so you *are* awake?" he said continuing. "Jen, I know how you think . . . there's nothing to wonder about."

I didn't need to wonder. Shawn spoke love to my spirit.

The week before Shawn died, I took Madelynn to a routine doctor appointment. Before we left for the checkup, I was calculating the deductible on our insurance.

"I'm trying to see if our city-employee health savings rolls over from year to year," I told him. "If I combine some appointments, maybe that would help."

"It's not worth stressing about," Shawn told me, and looked in the fridge for something to drink.

"It would be nice to save some money if we can," I said.

"But with hospital bills from the pregnancies, and little kids who always need to see a doctor for something, that savings account is always going to be used up from year to year, Jen."

"So you're saying that what I'm doing is a waste of time?" I asked.

"I'm just trying to *save* you time," he replied.

"Fine," I said as I bunched up the papers on the table and slapped them on a pile. I gathered up the kids, the diaper bag, my purse, and car keys. "I have to go or we'll be late. It's obvious my attempt to help us was a bad idea. I'm sorry I even tried."

"Jen . . ." he said and reached for my arm.

But I wasn't interested in continuing the discussion. I left in a hurry and drove to the clinic fuming, not even knowing what I was really mad about. Shawn had a point—we did use up our deductible savings each year. Still I wanted him to appreciate my efforts. Why was I so sensitive?

Preoccupied, I balanced both kids as the pediatrician told me that Madelynn was healthy and happy. That was my diagnosis as well. Good money spent.

After the appointment, I drove to my mom's house. I'd never done this before as my solution to a disagreement with Shawn. But I wasn't ready to talk to him quite yet. Cynthia was with Mom and they were delighted to see Jordan and Madelynn. I made up something about how we were in the area and wanted to say hi. I never mentioned anything about Shawn, but within thirty minutes I was impatient to get home.

Bringing the kids inside, Shawn broached the subject first. "I'm sorry. The insurance issue is not something to argue about."

I sighed. "I'm sorry for overreacting."

"I do appreciate your attention to detail. I can see why you'd be upset—trying to do something good for us and I counter it."

He was good at validating feelings. "Well, you had a point, too."

"I don't want to fight with you, Jen," he said. "We're on the same side."

"We're getting pretty good at working things out. This is better than not speaking to one another for days."

"Yeah," he agreed with a relieved grin and engulfed me in a hug. "Just think—soon we'll have this fighting thing down to less than five minutes."

This, I think, is how love is created—over time, with lots of nuances and patience and choices. It's built through many interactions, many times of saying *I'm sorry* or *I understand.* It's put together by many hugs, many silences, many kisses, and many conversations, even the ones that don't have words.

And in the end death makes the complex clear. We complicate the simple. It is our choice.

Love is a choice. This was Shawn's and my position on love. Just days after his death I journaled by a nightlight on the floor of my room:

This was our philosophy: Love is not a feeling.
I choose each day to wake and love you. I choose
to love you even when I don't feel like loving or
giving or helping or serving. I am committed to the
relationship. I'm dedicated to making it all God
intended it to be.

*I don't feel like I need a marriage. I feel capable.
I feel competent. I feel able. I feel like God has
been my strength and He continues to be my strength.
Therefore, the question is not a question about need.
I want to be in my marriage. Two healthy,
capable people, made better together.*

*I believe that love chosen out of complete desire
and surrender is stronger than love chosen out of need
or fear or insecurity. We risked everything for the sake
of the relationship. We risked our pride. We risked our
hidden agendas. We risked having to "be right."
We risked loving even if love would not be returned.
We risked greatly in order to love greatly.*

*This is the power of a life that has found love.
This is the example of something greater than ourselves.
This is the parallel of God's love for us. This is how I
know God is true. This profound love is a mere glimpse
of something God created to be everlasting. God's love is
complete. God's love is not a product
of emotion or mood or sentiment. God's love is about
choosing. God chose to love us. Will we love God?*

Love is our choice.

What happens when losing love isn't a choice? I'd never thought about love being taken away. The Bible says that love does not fail. Love is kind. Love is patient (1 Corinthians 13:4–8). But where had love gone? What was my world without Shawn's love? Losing my husband felt like the world had failed me—completely unkind and harsh.

Absolutely wrong.

Shawn and I had tried to stay away from absolutes such as using the word *always* in our conversations or disagreements. *You always stretch the truth. You always look at the negative. You always make us late.* Rather, we made an effort to work on the present situation: *You seem to be exaggerating a bit this time. Is it possible you're looking at this more critically than usual? Today for the birthday party, we were late. How can we change that?*

After his death, I found myself constantly wanting to use absolutes. *He always listened. He was always patient. He always communicated well. He was the strongest man.* Shawn, though, was the first to admit his imperfections, and if he'd heard me, he'd probably correct me. Okay . . . so *He listened often. He tried to be patient. He worked to communicate well. He was the strongest man I ever knew.*

But . . . he *always* loved me. That I knew was absolute. That he always loved me proves that some things on earth are conclusive, definite, and untouched by death. He always loved me.

The greatest significance Shawn's life played by intersecting a few short years with mine was, without question, to show me love in its purest form. He loved me through my vulnerabilities and my failings. He saw my heart bared, and loved even what I believed to be my weakest, most ugly parts. He loved the real me.

His love is irreplaceable, invaluable, and inconceivable. Even in loss, I feel Shawn's love driving me to keep going, to believe in a love that is everlasting, and to trust there is something more. Death failing to extinguish love is a sign to me that Christ's love is real. God's love does not fail. God's love always remains.

A reoccurring theme in my reflections on his death was the fact that Shawn didn't take anything with him to heaven. Not his computer or favorite pair of khaki pants, no headaches, stress, pain, to-do lists, or regrets.

The only things Shawn took with him as he crossed from earth to heaven was his faith, his hope, and his love. "And now these three remain: faith, hope and love. But the greatest of these is love" (1 Corinthians 13:13). Love crosses the barrier of time. Love has remained.

Like a rich satin stain brings out the grain in wood, loss gives me new insight into love. Love is everlasting. Love isn't bound by time. Shawn's love is a gift God gave me to keep.

My counselor summarized, "You grieve deeply, because you love deeply. And you wouldn't miss what you didn't love. You're conflicted because while you're hurting, you know this kind of pain is also a privilege—to know a love that gave without reserve and was responded to by every part of you. That's an amazing gift on this side of heaven."

Love remains. This truth nurtures and sustains my heart. In my memories of Shawn I am again able to feel his love. Love is related to something eternal. This unwavering love—a huge comfort in the midst of the unsteadiness of grief—contributes to the healing process. Love never dies (1 Corinthians 13:8 MSG). When I think about the love I shared with Shawn and that it will stay with me as long as I live, I am filled with hope for finding meaning in life. There is a link between love and significance.

Shawn's love will sustain our children as well. Their father loved them completely, and that will remain with them as they grow older. So not only did Shawn's love touch us in the moment, it also makes a mark for the rest of our lives.

God created us to practice love in our daily lives. Love is woven into our hearts. Because love, indeed, remains within us, the love we give or receive is significant—any time we choose to love, any time someone chooses to love us. Giving and receiving love builds the relationships we continue to value in our lives and essentially deepens our faith walk.

Interactions done in love are both far-reaching and enduring. The love that is shared on earth will be understood in full in heaven. God designed love to be an ongoing, central blessing of our lives as his love and the love of those he brings to us strengthens and encourages us.

In a support group I learned to outline what I'd lost, what I still had left, and what was yet possible. Love motivated me. I sensed a new reassurance that I could live without Shawn—not because I want to or wish to or would have ever chosen to, but by the grace of love, I am sustained. I am still alive for a reason. Does this make losing Shawn easier? No. Does it help me to start seeing new possibilities? Yes.

Love transcends. The love Shawn showed me was a glimpse of the same love God shares with me—the love God has for all of us. How do we know God loves us? Does God care? Does God feel our pain? John 3:16 (NLT) says that "For God loved the world so much that he gave his one and only Son, so that everyone who believes in him will not perish but have eternal life." Moved by his love for us, God gave us the gift of life by sacrificing his Son.

For me, the most striking part of this particular Bible passage is often overlooked. God *lost* his son! If anyone knows what it is like to lose someone you love—God does. God experienced tragic loss and the package of grief and sadness that comes with death. God knows my pain because he went through the deepest nature of hurt and separation.

Consider a friend asking you to travel cross country on a long and treacherous road trip, one with late nights, much discomfort, and little rest. In fact, your friend isn't even quite certain of the final destination but she desperately wants a companion for the ride. This is your very best friend and she has done countless things for you. You aren't extremely interested in the expedition, but you would do anything for your friend so you decide to go.

Why do you go? Because you care. You care for the overall well-being, needs, and request of your friend. So you go. Your presence is your strongest indication that you care.

"Be strong and of good courage; be not frightened, neither be dismayed: for the Lord your God is with you wherever you go" (Joshua 1:9 RSV). Why does God journey with us? Because he cares for us. Like a very best friend, he comes near our pain and wants to walk beside us in our hurt.

In a 2007 Washingtonpost.com religion post, Archbishop Emeritus Tutu, who was awarded the 1984 Nobel Peace Prize for his work with racial injustice, wrote, "Our God cares, for this God is Immanuel, God with us, who joins us in our dumbfounded speechlessness and bewilderment and this God does not give advice from a safe distance but enters the fiery furnace of our anguish and God wipes away our tears, this God who knows us by name, from whom nothing, not even death can separate us."

Nothing can separate us from the love of God (Romans 8:38–39). God wants us to know of his immense love, and to journey in this life toward the purpose and love he has destined for us. "The LORD will fulfill his purpose for me; your love, O LORD, endures forever" (Psalm 138:8). God created us to know him. There is a reason we are here. We have something to contribute. I was able to move toward healing when I became convinced there was still a reason to live. This is testimony of how much God cares and loves me.

God is guiding us to look for the unseen, for something that lies beyond. *The Message* Bible clarifies the concept of love in this way: "But for right now . . . we have three things to do to lead us . . . . : Trust steadily in God, hope unswervingly, love extravagantly. And the best of the three is love" (1 Corinthians 13:13).

Faith, hope, and love—three words of healing. But can you have either authentic faith or eternal hope if you don't have love? Will we accept God's mighty love? We are all invited to make a choice. God leads us when we are severely broken. "God is love" (1 John 4:8). Love leads us to healing.

God wants to heal us by filling our lives with love. "And I pray that you, being rooted and established in love, may have power, together with all the saints, to grasp how wide and long and high and deep is the love of Christ, and to know this love that surpasses knowledge—that you may be filled to the measure of all the fullness of God" (Ephesians 3:17–19). I picture my life alive with love, drenched in love, covered in love, a safeguard around me and around those I love, a promise for how my heart will heal. God wants us to live full lives of love.

How does God fill the void of loss when our lives don't feel full? Action is imperative. To disengage from life leads to doubt and despair, where it's impossible to heal. After Shawn died, my lack of movement further immobilized me. I closed down. I wanted to stop living. Nothing seemed to matter.

Love is necessary for survival. Love nourishes. Love is the pivotal link that connects us to a meaningful life. When we engage with the world—forming a new relationship, nurturing an established friendship, experiencing the beauty of God's nature, or delighting in trying something new—God is working his love through us.

When we are part of a loving relationship—whether it is with a spouse, a sibling, a parent, a child, or close friend—we have confidence. Our incompletes feel more balanced. Our insecurities are safely sheltered. Although our earthly relationships can never be perfect, they provide assurance, companionship, and intimacy.

In 1 Corinthians 16:13–14 Paul writes, "Keep your eyes open, hold tight to your convictions, give it all you've got, be resolute, and love without stopping" (MSG).

Love restores. Love is present-minded. Love keeps going. Love looks for the best. Love concentrates on the now, and how to share in the moment. Love does not give up. Love searches and finds the truth. Love completes us.

Love's completing us is the small-scale version of the larger picture with our heavenly Father. Unencumbered by human faults, he completes us fully, where others have failed. How much greater is a loving relationship with God? God's love is untainted, pure, and absolute. God's love knows no bounds. There is no better healing than in the arms of love that make us whole—the arms of God.

It is from this place of enduring love that we can begin to trust our Creator and find the resilience to keep moving. That even in my depths of pain he wants the best for me.

Jennifer and Shawn the summer before he died.

Wedding day, May 12, 2000 (Photo by Tane Finely. 2000. Used by permission.)

Peace Corps days stationed in Honduras 2001–2003 with travels to Machu Picchu, Peru.

One of Shawn's many loves and passions—photography.

Left: Jordan (born December 18, 2003) with his daddy.

Below: Madelynn (born April 8, 2005) with her daddy.

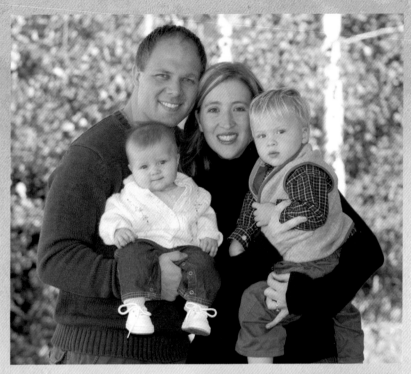

Above: Family photo
taken three days before
Shawn was killed.

Right: Last photo
Shawn ever took of
Jordan and Madelynn.

Inset: Funeral procession, September 12, 2005 (Photo by Dana Hennen. 2005. Used by permission.)

Below: The locker (Photo by Lisa Slotsve Photography. 2006. Used by permission.)

Shawn's mom, Bonnie Silvera, and Jordan.

Maddi meets President George W. Bush at the Law Enforcement Memorial Dedication (Photo by Jennifer Johnson. 2005. Used by permission.)

Jordan wears his daddy's badge with honor in Washington, D.C., in May 2006.

Jordan and Sergeant Bill in Washington, D.C., May 2006.

Jesus encouraged his listeners to fully trust in God: "If God gives such attention to the appearance of wildflowers—most of which are never even seen—don't you think he'll attend to you, take pride in you, do his best for you? What I'm trying to do here is to get you to relax, to not be so preoccupied with *getting*, so you can respond to God's *giving*. People who don't know God and the way he works fuss over these things, but you know both God and how he works. Steep your life in God-reality, God-initiative, God-provisions. Don't worry about missing out. You'll find all your everyday human concerns will be met" (Matthew 6:30–33 MSG).

I believe God's love walked me through the honest, naked, difficult grief process. Faith, hope, and especially love broke the bondage of the earthly traps of pride, jealousy, arrogance, vanity. Love beckoned me to stay strong, keep going, hold on, and not give up. And true to my long-standing belief—love is work. Healing through love is very hard work. Still, absolutely worthwhile. Love encourages the heart to be whole again in the most everlasting sense.

On the second anniversary of Shawn's death I woke up expecting the day to be similar to all previous 729 days I had survived without him. Empty. I didn't think it would be a bad day. I just predicted it would be another day of adapting. The day would be busy, keeping my mind preoccupied. It was Jordan's first day of preschool. I had a haircut appointment and in the evening we had plans to meet at the gravesite with family and friends.

I hurried into my room to make my bed, hang up clothes, and get ready for the 6th of September. I looked at my nightstand and noticed the drawers opened with a few things scattered. Somewhat exasperated I wondered why my children find it necessary to continually make my bedroom a favorite place to explore and play. Approaching the dresser to tidy up the mess I glanced on the bed. Our Couple's Bible, one I had not used since Shawn died, lay open there, with a letter propped on it. It seemed to be purposely placed for me to find.

I stared in disbelief. Tears welled. I held it with care and read the words "1st Anniversary Letter" again and again. I imagined Shawn nudging our children, instructing them to "help Mama find her note."

I had searched frantically for this very letter, which had been misplaced in our move back from Honduras. My friend Andrea had told me, "You will find it when you need it most." I finally had to stop looking, and just trust.

Standing now, with the letter in hand, two years to the day after Shawn's death, I whispered, "The time is now." God showed up. God may not be on my time schedule, but he is never late.

I decided to open the letter at the end of the night. I wanted it to be the last part of my day—alone where I could concentrate on every word and let the message sooth me.

Dearest Jennifer—

It truly amazes me how blessed I am and have been since we married one year ago. I think back on the chaos of my life and the calm that you have brought. Words cannot express the transformation of spirit I have experienced. You are my light and my love; my North Star. As I sit here on this rock breaker, in Canada, with a 40°F wind whipping at me, my fingers grow numb, but my heart warms me knowing you are mine and I am yours. I pray that time and circumstance allows us to read these when the time comes (5-12-2025). Happy 25th Anniversary!

The first year of marriage has been a challenge. I remember the first 3–4 months of simply adjusting to living together. The rule we came up with about "we always sleep together at night even if we are mad, hurt, or fighting."

The monthly month-a-versaries celebrating our marriage every month (what a great idea). Applying for the Peace Corps, meeting Laura y Jorge Jeandet, growing

*spiritually together, traveling to California, Chicago,
D.C., Mexico, and the many lessons in patience and love.*
    *This first year I have learned a lot about you, love,
and patience. At times I have had to fight the urge to
just run away when your will and what you wanted
dominated our relationship. But we both have areas to
work on and I always came to the same conclusion, love
is a choice. Each time I have chosen love. There is not a
day that passes in which I do not feel like I love you more
than the previous day.*
    *I am so excited to see what God has in store for our
futures. I pray he would bless us, and bless us a lot! You
inspire me and instill in me a drive to be a better person.
With you I am content!*
    I love you,
    Shawn

After reading the letter I sat in the shimmer of peace. Instead of missing him more I was loving him greater. I felt an astounding assurance in our relationship. How strong and right we were for each other. There is true inner peace in a life that lives without regrets. On a night where I could easily find myself stuck in grief at the two year anniversary or hopelessly yearning for the past and feeling sorry for myself, the letters of love gave me security and hopefulness. I felt free. I felt the freedom of a life lived well, a life loved deep, and a relationship founded on faith in Christ. It is all connected. Shawn's love for me parallels the love God has for me. And it is God's perfect love that heals me, holds me, and ultimately frees me.

    So, you believe in love? The voice was gentle with me.

    Yes I do. I believe in love, I declared.

PART FOUR

HOPE

I always believed God had great plans for my life . . .
I believe that once again with a new fervor.
I know it is sometimes hard to see what God is doing in
our lives . . . as the changes can be so subtle.

FROM SHAWN'S ANNIVERSARY LETTER TO JENNIFER
May 12, 2002

CHAPTER 11

Live a Preferred Life

I know what it is to be in need, and I know what it is
to have plenty. I have learned the secret of being content
in any and every situation, whether well fed or hungry,
whether living in plenty or in want. I can do everything
through him who gives me strength.

—PHILIPPIANS 4:12–13

preferred the life I had with Shawn over anything else. For a long time after he died, I wondered if I would ever prefer anything different in my life again. When we had been together, I never woke up wishing the day away or hating my life. Life was life. I mostly enjoyed it and never had reason to plot for escape. After he was gone, I woke up morning after morning with heaviness in my gut—dispassionate about the day in front of me. For the first time in my thirty-plus years, I was living a life I didn't want anything to do with.

> *If I close my eyes, I can feel your hand on the small of my*
> *back and remember the tiniest movement between us.*
> *Like an injured soldier feels phantom pain after a limb*
> *is amputated, I feel your touch, and my body begs you to*
> *come back. Return me to the motion of life. I never could*
> *have imagined life without you. Please come home.*

The whole process of grief is completely blurred, like driving in a rainstorm so heavy the windshield wipers can't keep up with the downpour. It seems dangerous to keep driving, but the urge to get home is stronger than the rain. I want to be home. I've been floundering long enough. I want to find a place where I can be content.

If I can't find that place, then I need to find the place closest to it. Writing is my closest place to home. Whether I'm typing late at night in my basement office or traveling across country for a writing retreat, writing has a curative, calming effect on me.

On my way to a retreat, I was stranded in the Minneapolis airport with a three-hour delay. I grabbed my laptop and found a restaurant that was nearly empty, its tiny tables nonetheless crowded together.

Waiting to order breakfast, I was distracted by people-watching: business people rushing to make a flight and tourists scurrying to find a gate, families trying to stay in a group, kids who had to go pee, babies crying over the commotion, and parents fighting due to all of the above.

As I watched these strangers, I wondered about their lives. I wanted to approach them and ask, "Don't you know what's happened to me? Do you know anything about death? How can you go to Disney World when my small-world-after-all is lost?" And to the couple fighting, I wanted to scream, "You don't have time for that! One of you could be gone tomorrow."

I was stirred out of my crazy fit when the waitress brought my coffee and took my order. Two minutes later she returned to seat a young businessman next to me. I stirred my coffee trying hard not to make eye contact. I didn't want to talk to anyone. Staring at my computer, I pretended to focus on work.

"Where're you going?" he asked.

"Phoenix," I replied. Maybe one-word answers would drop a hint.

"What takes you there?"

I never was good at dropping hints.

"I'm writing a book," I told him without thinking. *Why did I tell him that?* I cringed. *Can't I ever lie or make up an alias?* This was not the way to end a conversation. I knew his next question before it was asked.

"Oh? May I ask what your book is about?" Just then the waitress returned. I waited as he folded the menu and asked for the special.

"Well it's about . . . a life experience," I told him. I summarized my story and how Shawn had died. He listened intently, shaking his head.

"I've never been through anything like that," he said. "How do you get through it?"

"Honestly? Many days I'm not sure I am," I replied. "Writing is my therapy."

"That's good. I'm glad you found that. So what's your vision? Where do you hope to be two years after the book?"

I was surprised by the scope of his question. I didn't really have an answer.

"I hope to . . . be closer to . . . acceptance. It's a daily challenge for me . . . to accept . . . to accept this is real," I said, stumbling over my words.

"I can't even imagine," he replied. "What do you miss most?"

Another thought-provoking question. This guy was good. But out spilled the words I hadn't realized were bothering me until I said them. "I miss having someone to check in with. I miss coming to the airport and having that one person to call and say, 'I'm still here. My flight was delayed. I'll call you when I land. Love you.'"

My new acquaintance nodded. I felt like I was in a therapy session. The waitress returned with each of our orders and, without interrupting, placed the food on our separate tables.

"I miss having someone who cares," I added.

"That's tough," he said. He couldn't stop shaking his head.

"I was accustomed to my husband being interested in my life . . . Now a lot of the mundane goes unnoted . . . and sometimes even the exciting."

I wondered why I felt at ease talking with this man, and was surprised that this stranger didn't mind talking about death.

"How long were you married?" he asked.

"Five and a half years . . .

"Let me guess," he interrupted, "high school sweethearts."

"Yeah . . . I knew him for sixteen years. Basically half my life," I replied.

"That'll take some time getting over," he said.

"I'll never get over this," I said, certain. "It's now a part of me."

"It defines you," he suggested.

"I guess you could say that. Grief definitely defines a person . . . but I'd like to think I define how I respond to my loss. At some point I need to decide where I'm going with it." I wondered if this concept was too deep to be sharing.

"Of course," he said with another nod. The waitress refilled his coffee and put a slip on each of our tables.

"It's Valentine's Day tomorrow," I said, hoping to change the subject.

"I know," he said and lowered his voice, as if he didn't want to be reminded. "It's not exactly a holiday I'm celebrating this year."

I must have looked confused, because he offered an explanation. "My wife had an affair with our neighbor. We're separated . . . but trying to work it out for the kids."

"Wow," I said, displeased by my earlier assumption that the strangers walking by me couldn't hurt like I hurt. Perhaps everyone is fighting some type of battle. "I'm sorry. That's a heavy story too."

"Well . . . it is what it is," he said. "I don't believe in fairy-tale relationships or soul mates. There's probably more than just one person out there who's perfect for each of us."

His response didn't hide the longing in his voice.

"I don't believe in fairy tales either," I told him. "But I do believe Shawn was my soul mate. He was the one I liked coming home to."

"The most profound thing you mentioned," said the man, "was the part about having someone to check in with—someone who cares." We'd both finished eating, and he now gathered up his briefcase and overcoat. "That about sums it up. It tells me exactly what you lost. And I'm sorry for that."

I gave a weak smile. Pushing in his chair, he took both bills off of our tables and handed them, along with his credit card, to the waitress. "I got both of these," he told her.

"Thank you," I said.

With a final nod he replied, "Not a problem. I'm off to find my gate. Best to you with your writing." Then he waved and headed to catch a flight back home to a person he no longer checked in with.

I wondered how many people were like me and the businessman, who move through the world searching for hope. How many have lost something, how many want to be cared for? How many want something they don't have, or would prefer a life other than the one in front of them, but don't know how to get it?

Could I ever find a preferred life again—one in which I'd wake up in the morning and not want to swap my day with someone else? Could I find contentment? Could I find desire for a new life, my new life, that was still waiting to be created?

I had known both contentment and discontent. I prefer the former. The latter I can describe easily—a restless, unsettled state. Contentment is more difficult to define. Is it a choice or a circumstance? Is it something we control or something we come across?

The first time Maddi buckled her car seat by herself, she giggled proudly. I caught myself glancing up, wearing an "Isn't she cute?" expression, but no one was on the receiving end. It was the kind of look I would have given to Shawn, but now the glance was incomplete.

How can I explain it? The incident seems so minute, yet to me incredibly noteworthy. The feelings are a mixture of intricacies—pride, delight, dissatisfaction, melancholy, amusement. Anticlimactic. These glances may occur multiple times within a given day. It's habit. I look up and he isn't there, and still the habit persists.

I wrote that night in my journal,

> *She's changing from my lovable baby into my sweet*
> *toddler. She is precious. And I am privileged. Sometimes*
> *I wonder why I was given the gift to be her mom. She is*
> *my sight, my treasure, my heart.*

The next morning, I called Shawn's mom to schedule some "grandma" time. Jordan was jumping off his bunk bed, landing like a gymnast on the floor. My mother-in-law could hear the thump in the background.

"Is that Jordan?" she asked.

"Yes, he's doing lots of stunts. His latest is jumping off high towers by leaps and bounds."

"Well, that's Shawn," she said. "When he was in middle school he'd jump from the floor onto the island countertop in our kitchen in one leap!"

"That sounds like him," I said.

"He was so active," she told me. "That's where Jordan and Maddi get it. He's in them."

"I know," I replied. *But if he's there why do I so keenly feel his absence?*

Contentment and discontentment were wrapped up in the same package—loving my kids, missing their dad. *What is the opposite of complete? Lacking? Empty? Unfinished? Too many shortened exchanges.*

While we were dating, Shawn and I discussed that if we relied on each other for absolute happiness we'd be severely disappointed. We all have shortcomings, and we admitted it would be impossible to make the other entirely happy all of the time. We could, indeed, be a *source* of happiness for each other, but total fulfillment only comes from God.

Grief doesn't engage in lofty philosophies though. I argued with myself that Shawn *did* make me happy. I *was* content in our marriage. And I would take fulfillment with him any day—even with our imperfections—rather than go through this maddening separation. One widower told me, "I'd rather live our worst day together for the rest of my life than to be without her."

A handful of people have asked me if I'd consider remarrying. Some advised remarriage as a solution to my broken heart. I found this suggestion absurd. Yes, I pray that I will one day remarry, because I honor and respect the covenant of marriage and long for the companionship of being with someone. But remarriage is not a remedy for the pain of losing Shawn. I hope to remarry again to share in a whole and healthy and giving relationship, not as a Band-Aid to fix my hurt.

Further, the suggestion to remarry seems to make the wrong link—

that marriage *makes* one happy, rather than marriage contributing to happiness. There is a false belief in our culture that if we're miserable, someone in a new relationship will make us better. When the relationship fails to cure our misery, we're bitterly disappointed.

One counselor advised that I write out all the negatives of my relationship with Shawn so that I could ready myself for a new life and new relationship in the future. This assignment held a great disconnect for me. Why couldn't I validate my loving, vibrant relationship with Shawn *and* find new ventures and desires in my life? Why manipulate the truth?

This approach to therapy is like going on a fun vacation and then coming home with a list of all the trip's imperfections in order to be open to having a good time on the next vacation. Can't one enjoy both Tuscany and Florida? Both places have pros and cons. We don't need to denigrate one trip in order to enjoy a future one.

I would like to believe that we can have both—a loving past relationship that we remember with affection and a new life journey that will offer other beautiful pieces to love and learn from. Instead of writing off our past, we should authenticate the role it has played in our life. Tell the truth, which will free us—open us—to a remarkable future.

What, then, truly provides wholeness? What if we, as widows or widowers, never remarry? How can we be complete again? How can we find contentment? For me these are frightening questions because it isn't easy nor often preferred to walk through life alone.

I found the answer hard to grasp: only God, who created me to be whole in him, can make me whole again. I fought against this conclusion. *God,* I wondered, full of doubt, *can you fill me up? Can I be whole without Shawn? Will I ever be content inside my new life? Will you walk with me? Because even after three years, I'm not convinced I can do this. But I do want to try.*

It came to me that the first step in finding contentment is to identify what, apart from being without Shawn, makes me most discontent. What are the barriers to a contented life? Commotion. Comparison. Perfectionism. Complaining. Control. Hurt.

The entire world is full of commotion, busyness, distraction. Don't we all have something that pulls us away from contentment or leads us astray from what really matters? Tempts us? Causes us to wander? Maybe it's a demanding schedule, or eating comfort food, or lack of sleep, or a neglected friendship, or an obsession.

I was so torn up by my loss that I would go for days or weeks on marathon adrenaline. I wouldn't allow my body to rest or sleep for more than four to five hours a night. I rehashed my pain late at night when no one could see me. I was distracted by grief. I couldn't think of anything else.

The result? Many areas of my life were breaking down. I couldn't function at the energy level needed to mother my children. Healthwise my body did not have the daily amount of rest required to recover and renew. This made it nearly impossible for me to lose the extra ten pounds I had gradually gained back after drastic weight loss immediately following Shawn's death. My yo-yo weight issue added to my discontent and feelings of defeat.

My immune system was depleted, leaving me susceptible to various illnesses and repeated colds. Emotionally and mentally I wanted to give up.

One day I was talking to Karissa on the phone about how physically sick I felt.

"This is not your fault," she prefaced, "but I have to tell you that you're not getting enough sleep."

Defensive, I asked, "When am I supposed to sleep?"

"I know it's not easy. You have so much going against you. But, please try. I'm concerned for you. I think you've reached your lowest point of depression."

And she was right. I couldn't deny it. My entire body sensed how poorly I felt.

It's dangerous to live in the land of comparing—coveting a neighbor's life, a best friend's family, or the circumstances of a stranger at the grocery store. It's easy to do, yet rarely beneficial. And whatever story we make up in our minds, we don't know what that stranger's today is like or what their tomorrow will be. The majority of us walk around with hidden hurts.

One evening, while singing at church, I was struck by the priest's homily. He encouraged us to put ourselves at the foot of the cross and talk to Jesus, honestly expressing how we want to know him better.

Sitting in the pew, listening, I stared at the crucifix while tears stung my eyes. In my heart I confessed, *Jesus, I want to know you better by just living my life. Help me to stop comparing what I don't have with what I think everyone else does have. I have to trust that you made me for a reason. I just want to live my life in front of you.*

Putting my jacket on after mass, I approached the priest to thank him for his message. "It was exactly what I needed to hear."

He looked at me, sincerely humble, and said, "Well then . . . that makes two of us."

Like Chanttel had told me the week before, "There's always someone whose situation is worse." We tend to compare our lives to others', thinking the grass is greener, when sometimes the grass is even drier, weedier, browner.

Ironically, a few days later a friend called and after catching up told me, "I wish I had your life."

Bewildered and skeptical, I asked, "Why?"

"Because you have such peace," she said. "You are living with such conviction and passion. I wish I lived one day like that."

I hung up the phone, still completely baffled. *How could my friend want my imperfect life?*

I competed for a perfect life. I wanted a life with the dad, the mom, the kids, the house, the car (or two), the church to go to, and maybe a dog.

There's a major downfall in striving for perfection in an imperfect world. I was strangling myself with unrealistic expectations—goals that couldn't be reached, ideas that couldn't be implemented.

Before Shawn died, I was caught up in appearance both social and personal, exhausted by trivial trials like taking hours to choose a paint swatch for our new home or belaboring a conversation for months. I was challenged by my own dreams of raising a flawless family. The truth is people aren't judging me as much as I think, there isn't much difference between latte-tan paint and cappuccino-tan paint, and everyone has a bit of dysfunction somewhere in their family.

After he died, I was crushed with questions: What if life doesn't offer its best? What if life isn't perfect? What if the furnace needs to be replaced? What if the kids need braces? What if I can't put everything in a box, make it neat and tidy? What if I can't pretend this is okay?

Striving for perfection only feeds anxiety. Authentic living does not revolve around a perfect plan. Life is far from perfect. My best hope, then, is for a contented life, not a perfectly planned one.

Complaining becomes an easy habit in the aftermath of tragedy. It is a natural tendency to look at the negative—to focus on what we lack, to criticize a situation or person—when our spirits have been crushed. And it isn't really a surprise why. It is a normal response when dealing with the loss of someone we love to find ourselves unenthusiastic about life.

However, living inside a world of complaints is not only destructive but potentially damaging for the long term. Instead of helping us heal, complaining hinders our healing. This is because complaining perpetuates discontent. It reinforces our restlessness, making it even harder to find meaning and promising joy in our lives.

I blamed my unhappiness on loss to the point that I couldn't have seen happiness if it were resting in my hands. Indeed, Shawn's dying will always sadden my heart. And I would have never *chosen* for him to die. But like I told the stranger in the airport, I *do* choose how I respond to his death.

Choices. Deuteronomy 11:26 says, "Today I am giving you the choice between a blessing and a curse" (NLT). We all have a measure of choice, but for those of us who walk the path of grief, daily choices carry an additional burden. Will we continue living? Will we choose to see the good? Will we enjoy our children, our families, our friends? Will we live well? Will we live at all?

The translation of John 10:10 in the Amplified Bible says, "I came that they may have and enjoy life, and have it in abundance (to the full, till it overflows)." Live a full life! *Enjoy* a full life!

Just because there are days we don't look for it, doesn't mean joy isn't there. We can choose to see the blessings. Can we also choose to *enjoy* the blessings? If we curse our day, it only adds to our troubles—it never takes away our hurt. I started to find that some of my deepest contentment was born out of despair, because from there I could distinguish what is most valuable in life.

At first I confused contentment with control.

A few months after Shawn died I dreamed we were chasing death, like a storm chaser, a researcher who tracks and studies dangerous weather.

In the dream, Shawn and I were at a party. He put his arm around my waist and whispered, "This is my last day here. I know I'm going to die today. I just don't know how."

"Maybe you're wrong," I pleaded. "Maybe you're not supposed to die today."

We left and drove down side streets. Shawn swerved to miss a car and speculated, "Maybe I'll be in a car accident."

"Maybe you're not supposed to die today," I repeated.

Around the corner we saw a gang of teenagers. One of the boys had a gun in his hand. Shawn casually commented, "Maybe I'll be shot tonight."

I panicked. "No, Shawn, maybe *you are not* supposed to die tonight. Maybe *you are not* supposed to die at all!"

Throughout the dream Shawn was confident, peaceful. I was the one appealing for some type of control.

I woke up, wishing I had control—control over Shawn's death, control over my happiness. But the reality is, I *don't* control my circumstances. I *do* control my choices.

I couldn't even control the grieving process. Hurdles that I thought I'd conquered kept popping up over and over again. I wasn't able to pass through sequential steps in a recommended period of time. I could only choose to keep trying.

Could I choose to live a preferred life? I know that I prefer to live life the best that I can. But can I find a life I want to be a part of? Can I walk through my days choosing to be engaged, connected, and moving within the reality I face? How do I do this?

I began searching for a preferred life by choosing to appreciate the one I had and enjoy the blessings inside it. Balancing things I need to do and things I prefer to be a part of replaces chaos with calmness.

I find it important to continue participating in extended family occasions, for example. But I prefer not to go to every gathering alone. So at times I will invite a babysitter or friend to accompany me to an event, help me prepare the food I was asked to bring, pack or unpack my car, watch my children. The added assistance allows me to better manage my time, enjoy the situation at hand, and possibly even relax. Other times I need to decline invitations to reinforce my value of family time for Jordan, Maddi, and myself.

I control what I can—remembering that not everything is within my control.

Hurt can block potential. Pain invades, interferes. It's easy to get lost in sorrow. In my hurt, I risked giving up a life of effectiveness for a life of uselessness. That would waste not only the talents and gifts I'd been given, it would lead to continued despair. One way to counter desolation and unlock potential is through giving and receiving encouragement, appreciation, and help.

One morning Maddi tried to load and start the dishwasher by herself. Jordan, three and a half years old at the time, quickly came alongside to coach his two-year-old sister. "Okay, Maddi," he said, "put the soap in this part. Now shut the flap, Mad-len."

She followed each instruction.

"Great job, Maddi!" he cheered. "What a great listener! Mom, let's all clap for Maddi!"

Madelynn beamed at her brother's praise.

I stared, impressed, recognizing the lesson of encouragement they were sharing. We all have hopes, ideals, and dreams; we all know someone who has hopes, ideals, and dreams. Giving and getting encouragement brings out the best in us, fosters confidence, promotes potential, creates possibilities. Isn't this the stuff of a preferred life?

I sent my financial planner a card one day thanking him and his staff for their continuous service. The next week, Mitch called to thank me for the thank you. He said it was exactly what he needed to read as he was in the midst of a difficult decision to open a second branch for his business. Even though he knew what he wanted to do, my card encouraged him to follow his instinct and reach for his ambition.

One day I told God I felt abandoned. Hours later the doorbell rang. My realtor, Sue, stopped by with a gift for my kids. She gave me a quick hug before running to her next appointment. Never had I heard God speak clearer. *You are not alone.*

After my aunt Peggy died unexpectedly at the age of fifty-six from a blockage in her arteries, my cousin Kristine flew from her home in California to Minnesota to visit relatives. At the end of our week together, she told me, "Spending time with you is another connection to my mom. She cherished family time and I now see why . . . it is a source of encouragement."

Late one afternoon two and a half years after Shawn died, I e-mailed my sister Dee in desperation: "SOS. Can you come over tonight? I am feeling beyond hopeless."

I'd spent the day sweeping cereal off the floor, sweeping up a glass that broke while doing dishes, sweeping my kids into the bathtub— twice: the first time for tattooing themselves with magic markers and the second time simply for eating supper. The salad I'd made for myself had also ended up on the floor.

The radio sang, "Somehow I'm gonna find myself . . ." and I slumped down on my kitchen linoleum wondering how that was possible. I was surprised to feel so low after so much time had passed. It felt like Shawn had died yesterday.

Dee's e-mail reply read, "Yes. What time? With kids or without? I could bring my kids to play with yours or just come alone."

She came alone.

"Why are we in this world?" I asked, after we'd talked and shared and wept. "What does it all mean? Why am I even trying to write a book? What am I doing here?"

Dee sat on the couch facing me, legs tucked under to get comfortable, chin propped up by her hand.

"I don't want to be a hypocrite," I said. "Look at me. I shouldn't be the one writing stuff for others. I'm not qualified to give hope. I can barely find it myself."

My sister kept listening.

"I don't want to live just filling up my time with projects and intentions," I said. "Does any of it really help?"

"I'm going to pretend that isn't a rhetorical question," Deanna said. I blinked at her.

"You've been answering your question for the past two hours," she said.

I didn't know if I wanted to hear her explanation.

"There is, indeed, a reason for your book and a reason to write it, Jen. The book is your answer—at least right now—to doing something that matters. The people who know what it's like to plead and plod through their own lonely canyons will want to read your book. The ones who have days like yours, crying on the kitchen floor, picking up Cheerios, and cursing God. The thing that gets us through our hurt is to help someone else. Like when Cindy came to make you whole-grain muffins last night. She wanted to do something nice for you. That's an amazing act of kindness, and it touched you."

Dee had helped me make a connection. She left a little before midnight, and even though I needed to sleep, I decided to journal. I needed to write it down so I'd have it for the next time I found myself sunken in front of my fridge with a toddler asking for a hug and chocolate milk.

Somewhere, while we're heaped on the floor, striving to collect ourselves, sits another mom sunken in her situation, determined to do the same. We're connected. God uses us to help one another. And choosing to help satisfies. The place of desolation is where we are put to the truest test—to choose to help, to choose to love.

God's Good Word had been quoted to me often. It wasn't always comforting, but it always held true: "I am certain that God, who began the good work within you, will continue his work until it is finally finished" (Philippians 1:6 NLT).

I asked God one day, "What do you want from me?" I wasn't expecting an answer. Does God really speak to us—in actual words?

Immediately upon my speaking, though, my thoughts sensed a response. Not in a loud, audible voice, but real and unmistakable: *Greet me in the morning. Say goodnight to me when you go to bed. Include me in your day. Make me a part of it. I want to help you do this. I am not just here to carry you through. I want to be in the middle of where you need me most. You try to do too much on your own. Let me start helping you. This is what I want not only from you, but for you.*

I thought then about how I need God to be my very strength in each part of my day. I thought about what I wanted out of my life:

> *At the end of any given day, I want the peace of mind to know that I am exactly where I'm supposed to be.*
> *I want to live in the simple: to live with smiles shared and love given, to feel like I've contributed to the day, even if my contribution feels small. I want to know that I am valued and cared for, and I want those I love to know that I value and care for them. I want to see the better side of life, not just the part that makes me cry, but the*

side of joy as well. I want to experience the moment and
recognize it as remarkable.

Most of all, when I go to sleep at night, I want to know
that I can rest—not only because I am tired, but because I've
lived my day well. I've lived the best I know how.

This is the preferred life.

One night I heard a clank as something fell onto the countertop in the kitchen. I dragged myself out of bed and trudged down the dark hallway to find the source of the noise—praying it wasn't anything serious. Sitting next to the toaster was the cap to an under-the-counter light that Shawn had installed when we first moved into our new home. Ignoring it, I went back to bed.

The next morning, Jordan hopped onto the counter while I stirred oatmeal on the stove. As I poured the hot cereal into bowls, Jordan jumped down, wearing a big, proud smile and announced, "Mom! I fixed the light. I like to fix things, Mom!"

I peeked under the cupboard and was astonished to see that he had, indeed, put the parts back together.

As I smiled at him with appreciation, he asked, "Are you happy now, Mom?"

"Yes," I said, "I'm very happy. You do a great job fixing things."

We admired his handiwork with the light cap and I told him, "Thanks, Jordan, for fixing our light."

He gave me a strong hug and in a singsong voice replied, "YOU'RE welcome!"

Then he let go of my neck and hopped up and down (he is constant energy).

Becoming serious again, Jordan looked up at me and said, "I think it'll fall down again. Then I'll fix it again."

"That sounds good," I told him.

So many things to fix, I thought. *So many things to fix—again.* So many parts of the grieving process that I felt I'd already been through only to be surprised when they returned, and I felt like I was starting all over.

Jordan was willing to put things back together again, was *expecting* it. I wanted to copy him. I wanted not only a willing heart but an expectant one—one that does not practice fear but is content.

My dear Jordan, how many times can we fix broken hearts?

I suspected my son would tell me, "We'll fix our hearts again and again. We won't give up. We'll expect to work hard. And in the end life will work again."

We who have suffered loss are living in different lives—never to be like they were. That's the sad part—that life can never again be what it was. The chosen part is that our lives can still be enjoyed and cherished.

There will never be a day where I say, "I prefer this life without my spouse." Still every day, I have the option to say, "I prefer today over any other day." I choose to make *today* where I place my best energy, my best effort, and my best concentration. Today is my only guarantee. I choose to prefer the life in front of me instead of being buried by the life behind me.

Life comes back. This is true. Slowly life is coming back.

I'm glad you sense life returning. The voice found me while I was putting away breakfast dishes.

I stared out the window, ready for the conversation in my mind.

Moment by moment, I see glimpses, I agreed.

What do you choose for this moment? the voice prompted.

I wish I were content with all this, I thought.

Each moment is a choice, the voice nudged.

I shrugged at my distraction, reached for the silverware and threw it all in the drawer without separating forks from knives from spoons. I didn't want to think about sorting things out. Who was this voice inside my head? God? My own imagination?

But even without trying, I sensed something trying to reach my spirit—not in a frightening way, but carefully.

The voice came near: *I am here to help you believe.*

I knew only God could do that.

CHAPTER 12

Be Here Now

*When I stand before God at the end of my life, I would
hope that I would not have a single bit of talent left, and
could say, "I used everything you gave me."*

—ERMA BOMBECK

Three days before Shawn's death, we went for a bike ride. It was a day
wrapped in sunshine, something to savor in September, when a day
often holds hints of winter.

An added delight—it was the first time I'd ever swapped babysit-
ting with another stay-at-home mom and this arrangement completely
charmed me. Shawn and I could enjoy two daylight hours kid-free.

I announced my plan. "We're going on a morning date!"

Shawn was downstairs in the office, shuffling papers from one side of the
desk to the other. He leaned back in the office chair, swiveling to look at me.

"I have to work at two o'clock," he told me, "and I have a paper that's
due Monday. I should also look at that wedding video one last time . . .
I'm hoping to give it to the Johnsons next weekend. And if I have time I
want to fasten the cabinet handles in the bathroom."

"I could still take the kids to Nancy's," I said, "and we could each do
our own thing this morning."

After thinking for a second he said, "No, that's okay. I'll work on this
paper Sunday night. Let's go for a bike ride."

Without a hint of regret, he put the computer to sleep.

I ran upstairs to change Jordan and Madelynn from pajamas to play
clothes, but within minutes Shawn was calling me from the garage.

"What is it?" I asked.

"The bike rack your dad gave us is made for his Saturn," he said. "It doesn't work so well on our Taurus."

"Well . . . if it doesn't work," I replied, "we don't have to go for a bike ride."

"Let me see what I can do," he told me.

I ran back upstairs, and ten minutes later Shawn called me to take a look. Our car was wrapped with several ropes and bungee cords devised to secure the bikes.

"This looks clever," I said.

"The car has a few more scratches on it than before," he felt obliged to tell me, "but the bikes should stay on." Taking Madelynn from my arms, he told me to grab some water bottles.

With both kids buckled in and bikes strapped on, Shawn backed out of the driveway. "Oh, by the way," he said, "my bike has a flat tire."

"Shawn," I said, putting my hands on the dashboard, "maybe we aren't meant to go on this bike ride today."

"It's no big deal . . . We'll just stop at the gas station to put air in the tire before we go. We need to get gas anyway."

We finally dropped off our kids, and set off on the bike trail.

"Let's ride fast to get good exercise," I suggested.

"Let's ride right next to each other," he said. "We never have time to just talk."

For the next forty-five minutes, pedaling up the trail and back, we talked about random things. We even took five minutes to stop at a garage sale.

When we returned to our car, I noticed there were no pedals on Shawn's bike—just pegs where special mountain-biking shoes clicked in place. In the whirlwind of getting ready that morning, he didn't have time to search for his shoes, which were still in a box somewhere from our move. He had worn his old, torn sneakers.

"How were you riding without pedals?" I asked.

"It's not that hard. I just have to balance my feet a bit," he replied.

"Well . . . thank you," I said.

"For what?" he asked.

"For going on the bike ride."

"I'm glad we did," he said.

Shawn had a knack for taking things in stride, for taking what the moment offered.

"What now?" he asked. "We have about fifteen minutes before we have to get the kids."

We'd parked next to the Nesting Grounds Coffee Shop, so I suggested we get coffee. Shawn nodded, fastening my bike behind his. Inside, he ordered a Turtle Mocha. By this point in our marriage I had learned that whatever the guy orders somehow always appears and tastes better. At restaurants I'd always ask to sample his meal, and even trade on occasion. Not wanting to waste time making a simple decision long, which I had a knack for, I knew it was safe to order a decaf of the same, since I was nursing Madelynn.

We sat in oversized leather chairs by a stone fireplace, and Shawn thumbed through a coffee-table book about Alaska. We hoped for our ten-year wedding anniversary to go on an Alaskan cruise.

Before coming in, I had grabbed a book from the car that I wanted to show Shawn: *Captivating: Unveiling the Mystery of a Woman's Soul* by John and Stasi Eldredge. I'd just finished reading it that summer.

Shawn grinned at the title and told me, "Well, the book must have worked . . . it's a mystery you could order coffee so fast today."

I ignored his humor. "There's a quote in it I like."

I found the page I was looking for and began reading about an elderly couple's motto for a good marriage: "The gentleman looked to his wife and asked, 'Do we have a family motto?' She answered, 'Well, it's been on the refrigerator for the past thirty years.' He asked, 'What? Amana?' After some laughter, this is what she shared—"

I paused. Shawn was chuckling. I looked at him blankly. "I don't get it," I said.

"Amana? Like Whirlpool," he replied.

"Oh!" I felt a bit silly. Sometimes it took me awhile to get a joke, even an easy one. "Good thing I have you to interpret this stuff for me!" I told him.

I picked up the book again only to find myself choking up. This surprised me. I knew the quote was motivational, but not necessarily emotional.

I handed the book to Shawn and said, "Here, you read it to me. You're strong and I know you won't cry."

Setting his coffee on the table between us, he took the book from my hand and started reading the selected section to me: "Now we should live while the pulse of life is strong. Life is a tenuous thing . . . fragile, fleeting. Don't wait for tomorrow. Be here now! Be here now! Be here now!"

"This is how I want to live," I told him.

"It's strong," he answered.

We both understood the message and found little that could be said to add to the meaning. I looked at his watch upside down. With less than five minutes to spare, we got up, threw away our coffee cups, and walked with arms linked to our car.

In that moment, time seemed irrelevant. But each moment leading up to that day, including the ones that had contained obstacles, brought us to a place where our spirits were connected—and I believe he felt it too. It was clear—"Be here now" was to be our new message for living.

Only three days after our bike ride, my husband was killed. Never again would we ride bikes together, order the same kind of coffee, or spend time pondering our life's philosophy.

Looking back, I wondered if somehow we knew that Shawn was soon to meet his Maker. Were our hearts being prepared? I'll wonder for the rest of my life. But this is what I do know. There is no misinterpreting the quotation I shared with Shawn that day. It was almost like a prayer over my life. I need to live *now*.

A few weeks prior to the bike ride, Shawn was sitting at the kitchen table. Without providing any context, he said, "Jen, I can't wait to go to heaven. It's going to be amazing."

I looked at him, startled and perplexed.

He caught my look and quickly added, "Don't get me wrong. I want to live with you until we're ninety. I just know that heaven will be awesome once we're there."

"I wish I was as sure as you," I said. "I'm scared to die, Shawn. I don't like thinking about it."

I had strong faith, but death, even heaven, was so unknown. How could he be so confident?

"Jen, we can't be afraid," he told me. "When our time is up, it's up. I can't sit and worry about when I'm going to die . . . I could die just as easily on my way to the gas station, the grocery store, or going to church."

I knew he was right. Our only guarantee is today. And even though I'm not sure how God prepares us for death, I do see how God prepares us for the present moment. God had been preparing my heart—shaping and molding, refining and polishing my character and my skills, each moment of my life building me for this present one.

In an e-mail, an old friend wrote, "God orchestrates our lives from our future." She explained that God knows where we need to be and when, and leads us rather than pushing or prodding from behind. Everywhere we go, each experience we enter and walk through, God is bringing us to the next place in his plan.

God is a good economist. He wastes nothing. Everything is used to fulfill his ultimate purpose in us. If, in God's economy, not a single moment of "now" goes to waste, then being in the now—taking note of it, making use of it—can't be insignificant.

Some days the message to live now is, in fact, the only thing that keeps me going. Believing that each moment contributes to a purpose allows me to breathe, live, and move. If I lose belief in meaning, then my spirit will slowly suffocate. It's the difference between functioning and completely breaking down.

Living now becomes my mission. I want to tell everyone I know about the power of its message. Still, it's a tremendous challenge, and I wonder if the God I believe in will protect me as I continue to waver. To live in the moment is a huge undertaking and although I've adopted it as my intent, I often want to rebel, "God, this can't be the plan. I liked the old one. Switch the plan. This one isn't working!"

A little over a year after Shawn died, our dear family friend and cheer-leader, Mary Jo, died unexpectedly at the age of fifty-two from a heart condition. After Shawn died, she was one of my truest comforters, always generous with help or a hug.

Like my dad always quoted from the poet Maya Angelou, "People will forget what you say, people will forget what you do, but people will never forget how you make them feel." Mary Jo had a way of making those around her feel like they could do anything. Her greatest gift, both in words and practice, was her vibrant personality that encouraged me not to waste a magical moment.

Making our moments magical, or even simply matter, isn't an easy assignment. I daily struggle with the depression that seeps into a void of what-I-wish-could-be. And there are occasions when I wish away moments altogether.

One evening I was flying home from a trip to Florida with my kids and my sister, Cynthia. Madelynn, both overly tired and excited to be on a plane, squirmed in my arms until I was utterly exhausted and begging her to sleep. Meanwhile, the man seated next to us watched with bulging eyes that scolded me to keep my child quiet.

The flight attendant announced that the individual overhead lights weren't working therefore the main cabin lights would remain on to accommodate the passengers who wished to read. Getting Maddi to rest under the bright lights would be impossible. The man next to me held his book closer to his face, obviously trying to block us out. For the duration of the trip, Maddi and I wrestled in our confined seat by the window.

For over two hours I prayed for the flight to end. The experience was like a nagging toothache, and I bargained with God for just two minutes of relief.

Then it happened! Maddi's eyelids drooped. Her eyes fluttered in protest. Once. Twice. She was asleep! I reveled in two whole minutes of complete quiet—or maybe it was four. I wanted to nudge the guy next to me and brag at my accomplishment, but he was wearing a travel eye-mask and a do-not-disturb sign over that.

As I studied my daughter's delicate features, I marveled at the gift of two minutes. The plane was already taxiing toward the gate but I drank in this seeming eternity of peace and pleasure—only an instant in reality. Holding my baby girl in my arms, I savored the treasure stored within a moment.

Is this what my husband's life, Mary Jo's life, had witnessed to me? Take the moment in stride, whatever it brings—savor the moments that matter as they come. Would the rewards of trudging through grief bring ultimate peace, even if I had to wait until heaven? Sometimes the beauty of a single moment is hard to see without the chaotic moments that lead up to it.

Each moment matters. Live them now.

The second year after Shawn died I worked with a life coach. She helped me see the possibilities outside my pain.

During one of our phone sessions, I told her, "I feel so overwhelmed. Whether I'm doing something productive or simply existing, I feel weighed down by grief."

"Can you allow yourself to be in the state of 'overwhelm'?" she asked.

"I've never thought about 'overwhelm' being a place," I replied.

"Explain how this place of 'overwhelm' feels."

"Heavy. I dreamed about Shawn last night. I can never catch him or catch up to him, and I wake up feeling like I've been running a marathon all night."

"Do you like to dream about him?" she asked.

"Yes. Always. I love to see him, and I can most vividly see him in my dreams."

"Tell me more," she said.

"I wrote in my journal this morning that the weight of grief is heavy . . . like water—a rushing kind of water, and I'm collapsing under it, drowning in it."

"Go on," she coached.

"The parallel of water works well with grief," I told her. "Like the rise and fall of tides, I go in and out of sanity all day long."

"So the drowning feeling matches the overwhelmed feeling you have."

"Exactly," I said. "How do I live in the moment when I'm engulfed by grief every time I try to focus on something new?"

I knew I was teetering on the edge—accepting a new way of living without Shawn and at the same time running scared from it.

"What's your answer to that?" she asked.

Don't you hate it when counselors throw the question back at you? I don't want to figure this out for myself. I want someone to hand me a solution. But we can't expect others to have our answers. We have to learn to trust our own.

After a moment of silence I replied, "I have to own my moments."

"I like that," she said. "Tell me what that looks like."

"Whether the moment is good or bad, it's what I have. I can't control life, death, or even the waves of grief," I told her, the ideas gushing out. "But I can take charge of how I'll make the most of today."

"And if you're in 'overwhelm'?" she asked.

"Then that's where I am. I'm more apt to save myself by treading water than by panicking." I pictured a woman thrashing in the water, her arms flailing, screaming to be rescued. "I either have to ride the waves or wade through them. I'll never save myself by going under."

"I think you're on to something," she said.

Our session was over too soon. We scheduled a time to talk the next week. After hanging up I stared at my calendar, thinking I had a lot to work on. God created me to be here now. It was up to me to live on purpose. I wrote some notes on the side of my planner:

> *Life lived with intention rises above life lived with indifference. It is the distinction between triumph and defeat, between losing a loved one and losing my entire self. It is a life that wakes up each day and says, "I will make something of the moment before me. I will celebrate now."*

This is my moment. This is your moment. Our lives have changed, and now our lives stretch us to prepare for something more.

It's a lot to own.

In the months after Shawn died I longed to hear his voice one more time. I prayed, "If only I could have one more conversation or share one more moment with my husband."

One day as I repeated this desperate prayer, God reminded me of our anniversary letters. This was the first time I'd thought of them since Shawn died. In his infinite grace, God had answered.

Racing upstairs to our bedroom closet where they were stashed in a shoe box, I untied the letters one by one, whispering in gratitude for the treasure before me. I was about to hear my husband's voice again. These were the letters we'd stockpiled—saved for an undetermined occasion.

Shaking with anticipation, I knew I couldn't open any of the letters right away. I wanted to relish each one, and the expectancy for the words they held would be such comfort. Reading them would be an occasion, at a special time in a special place.

The December after Shawn's death, I traveled with Deanna and her husband, Jim, back to Honduras. They offered to accompany me and help with the kids, making my children's well-being a priority as we traveled to a third world nation—a place I called my second home.

From the instant we stepped off the plane, familiarity returned. Dusty streets, stray dogs, clay-tile roofed houses, mango trees, and kids running barefoot. A flood of memories.

After greeting the villagers of the town that Shawn and I had come to know so well, I walked down to the river at the foot of the hill. There, I snuggled in the hollow of a huge crooked tree where Shawn had carved our initials. I'd already decided to open the letters in reverse chronological order—because I had misplaced year one—so, without a watch or any pressure to be elsewhere, I pulled out the letters dated May 12, 2005.

Dearest Jennifer,

Happy 5th Year! Another year and another child. As our family grows I'm reminded how blessed I am to have you as my wife. Two days ago someone asked me what you were doing for work: I told them that your main focus right now was raising our children, and you are a full-time mom. After I said that I reflected on the sacrifice you have made in your professional life in order to stay at home with our kids, and how by doing that we are in the minority. It also occurred to me that you took on this role with no complaining. I'm amazed that you work so hard every day doing repetitive tasks that I know must get old fairly quickly. I deeply respect your perseverance and commitment especially thinking about the years to come and how these tasks will only be repeated over and over the next five years of our marriage. You are an amazing woman and I love having you as the mother of my children.

As I start this new chapter in our lives with me going to school, my classes focus on the basics of healthy relationships, and there is a strong focus on teaching people key behaviors and key communication skills. Most of the skills mentioned, especially for couples, are familiar, as they are the same skills we discovered on our own while we were in Honduras. I love the security of knowing that there is no situation so far that we have not been able to work through and that there is never any need for us to "agree to disagree."

I'm not sure where we are headed, but I certainly enjoy the freedom you have given me to continue my education. Your support and encouragement has been the motivation I needed to do this. Thank you!

I look forward to the next five years and the adventures that are to come.

You continue to captivate, motivate, and inspire me. You are an amazing woman who moves in mysterious ways that draws me into a world I never would have known without you.

I "something" you!

Shawn

I had once said to a friend that my best therapy for healing came from Shawn himself. I knew he would want for me, I could hear his advice encouraging me to be here now and keep living.

His letter reinforced this envisioned guidance. I could see where he had lived the message of living the importance of today in everyday ways, whether it be at school or working on our marriage or spending time with our children or finishing the basement. And I realized that once those moments are past we can never bring them back. Death is permanent. Now we should live.

My letter echoed an idea to enjoy each moment.

Dear Shawn,

    Happy 5th anniversary! Can you believe we have been married five years?! When I was thinking yesterday about what I would write, the thought that came to mind was it just keeps getting better—you and me—life with you—our family. I love being with you.

    I look back on this year and think about where we've come from, where we are going, what we have accomplished, what we are dreaming to do! We have two kids now: Jordan and Madelynn. They are precious, beautiful children—our best creation. They give me purpose, joy, love, life, pleasure.

    You started school last month to finish your four-year degree in psychology. You are excited and motivated— and I'm extremely proud of you and look forward to seeing where God will take us with your initiative. We started a photo business this year. You are exploring and enhancing your knowledge in photography. I enjoy the creative side of putting together the details—meeting new clients and designing the proof books.

    It amazes me that we are able to work well together. It shows me the balance between our relationship and how we complement one another. I think we started to refine these qualities in Honduras—working through communication patterns, resolving interpersonal conflicts, discovering sensitive issues, and learning to overcome our weaknesses with patience, support, and love.

This is what excites me about being with you: working to make each year better—vesting our energy, time, strength, our raw selves; wanting, hoping, making a relationship that will be the most defining experience of our lives. Knowing that when we one day leave this earth to meet our Maker—we will be able to say—"I was a better person because of my love for Shawn and for the love he freely gave me.

"I lived the life planned for me—and I was able to reach my full potential because of the relationship God blessed me with. My marriage lived and breathed the example of Christ. Shawn showed me Jesus in a real, daily, and true way. He showed me the meaning of sacrifice and giving. He challenged me to soul search and find a loving, merciful, forgiving, grace-filled God."

My longing this year is to rejoice in the many gifts we have been given. I want to live in the moment and enjoy what the present has to offer. I often allow myself to focus on the past, question my decisions, worry with doubts, and hold on to regret. My prayer is that God will help me to move forward. Shawn, you are so good for me. You are tough—strong—solid—you stay the course. You are committed and faithful. You fight for what you want and for what is right. You rescue me from my fears.

I love you, Shawn.

Always—and if ever we should be separated—know I'll wait for you in heaven and know that my life was complete from having been your wife. You are all I ever wanted. God worked through you in my life—and for that I am not only a better person—but, eternally grateful.

Love, Jennifer

Shawn's letter speaks of an adventure. Mine reflects on a complete life lived through the present moment. Will I ever look back at my healing journey and define it as an adventure? A quest? Indeed, a life pursuit. One that began in love, remains in love, and is led by God's sustaining love.

This could be possible, I imagine, only by integrating loss and learning to recognize the moments in which to celebrate life. Then a day that feels like it couldn't possibly hold anything good has the potential to become a day that may, in fact, be one of our best.

What if today could always be our best day ever?

It says in Romans 12:1, "Take your everyday, ordinary life—your sleeping, eating, going-to-work, and walking-around life—and place it before God as an offering" (MSG).

This I can do.

Even on days when we have little to offer, something small can be given. Each motion, movement, interaction, conversation, contribution, assignment, chore, or tired hug holds meaning. God is just as pleased with us when we are still as when we are productive.

"I offer my best" has become my daily saying. I typed the phrase on several cards and hung it around my house—on my bathroom mirror, the diaper changing table, inside the shelf of my refrigerator, taped on the front of my computer, inside my sock drawer, tacked on the bulletin board above my phone, as a bookmarker on my nightstand.

Each day "my best" looks different. I don't pressure myself to make "my best" unobtainable. If showering or feeding my children is the extent of what I can offer, then I invest the best energy I possess to serve our three meals for the day with attention and care. I use these days to rest.

There are days I find inspiration to write or do something for myself and my kids: make a new recipe, go for a run, or explore a new park. Some days I commit to attending or speaking at a support group, cleaning the garage, or planning a wedding shower. Other days I get a massage or call a friend for coffee. I use these days to fill me.

Each day becomes my offering. And as I participate, I find that a sense of healing reveals itself in small, unpredictable steps. One evening my family volunteered to bag over ten thousand meals to be shipped to Haiti for relief. Driving home that night I thought *I can do this. I can offer a part of me. I can make a difference.* It felt good. And I wanted to experience that feeling again.

If we dedicate our moments to God, in turn those moments will become a blessing. We can offer him our ordinary, and he will receive it and cherish it.

On days that I follow the instruction to offer my best, peace comes. A soothing reassurance occurs when I allow the God of the universe to be the God of my moments. We shouldn't be surprised by this peace and reassurance. Throughout God's word, after all, he directs us to live the importance of *today* because he knows this manner of living fulfills us more than any searching or striving.

Philippians 4:4–8 encourages,

> Celebrate God all day, every day. I mean, revel in him! Make it as clear as you can to all you meet that you're on their side, working with them and not against them. Help them see that the Master is about to arrive. He could show up any minute!
>
> Don't fret or worry. Instead of worrying, pray. Let petitions and praises shape your worries into prayers, letting God know your concerns. Before you know it, a sense of God's wholeness, everything coming together for good, will come and settle you down. It's wonderful what happens when Christ displaces worry at the center of your life.
>
> Summing it all up, friends, I'd say you'll do best by filling your minds and meditating on things true, noble, reputable, authentic, compelling, gracious—the

best, not the worst; the beautiful, not the ugly; things
to praise, not things to curse. (MSG)

Being here now is a moment by moment practice—one that
doesn't happen without intent, one that has the potential to change
our lives. It's a daily commitment and discipline to practice the very
thing I want—a heart fully inhabiting the moment.

When I inhabit today, I engage and absorb what is around me. I
connect with life and often find my connections satisfying. When I hold
back—rehash my past or become anxious about the future—I inhibit
the moment at hand. I prevent and often forfeit the very thing I want.

Grief easily hinders us from living in the present. I struggle to stay
mindful of the *now*. I called Deanna and told her, "This concept to *be here
now* is too hard. I can't seem to remember the phrase when I need it most."

"Paint it on your wall," she said.

"What?"

"Paint it on your wall . . . or write it on your mirror with lipstick,"
she told me. "Like when you put all those 'I Offer My Best' signs everywhere—it reminds you."

That night I ordered a customized decal off the Internet to decorate
the wall above the patio doors in my kitchen-dining room. When it
arrived in the mail, my friend Cindy, from church, came over and spent
hours helping me adhere the words to my wall. In the end it read, as if
painted by hand, "Life is fragile and fleeting . . . be here now."

Clinging to each moment God gifts me is the only place where my
perspective stays clear and focused. First Corinthians 15:31 says, "I die
daily" (KJV). The word *die* indicates surrender. We are instructed to surrender daily. The practice to "be here now" teaches me to surrender my
wishes, wants, desires, and future dreams the way I'd conceived them
before Shawn died.

This is not abandoning hope for the future. This is not defeat or
helplessness. I continue to see great things in store for my life and the

lives of Jordan and Madelynn. Rather, to surrender means to begin living outside our own limited plans into God's purposed plan. There is only today to surrender our hurts, our headaches, and our heartaches in exchange for living fully.

Although I believe wholeheartedly in "be here now," the practice challenges me to the point where I often feel I'm failing miserably. It's easier to be consumed by pain, because pain is all consuming. But pain is not fulfilling. And the more I learn to live a life of moments that matter—being present-minded and thankful for simply moving—the more I see fullness being restored.

Today is our day to love our kids, extend grace to our families, give care to friends, or show concern for strangers. I found, by God's grace, that there are lessons upon lessons stored up in moments, waiting to have an extraordinary impact on my life. Like the weekend I was asked to speak at a marriage banquet and on the way to the event I called my sister to say, "I can't do this. I can't show up. I should be the last person to tell this group to *be here now*. I don't even know how to do it myself most of the time."

Deanna told me, "Then tell them that. People won't believe your message until they believe you are real."

Reluctantly I kept my commitment. I spoke to the group. I delivered my honest message of struggle. Afterwards several people approached me to share how my talk influenced them. Three marriage counselors told me I should consider a career in the field of marriage therapy. A woman who had recently suffered a miscarriage connected with my story and told me the idea of moving within loss encouraged her more than anything else she had read or tried.

And the best moment of the night? A couple who barely knew me came up and clasped a hand-crafted bracelet around my wrist etched with the word *Believe*.

On the drive home, after my hurried thoughts had reached their height, I let the interactions of the day calm me. Once in bed, I slept with great peace, my fingers twined tightly around the bracelet.

The next morning walking out to my kitchen to make coffee, I sensed God say, *I have a plan for today that involves you.*

That caught my attention like never before, and when I finally stood still, I heard the plan.

Trust.

I tried not to doubt. The message came stronger.

This is your moment to believe.

CHAPTER 13

Create Something New

*We look at this Son and see God's original purpose in
everything created. For everything, absolutely everything,
above and below, visible and invisible, . . . everything
got started in him and finds its purpose in him. He was
there before any of it came into existence and holds it all
together right up to this moment.*

—COLOSSIANS 1:16–17 (MSG)

D ays after Shawn died, Sergeant Bill brought me to the police
department to see Shawn's locker. He told me I would like it.
When we opened the locker door, I was stunned. All my notes!
All the lunchbox love notes were taped one after the other on the metal
door. The ones that Shawn had said were just "nice." He'd saved every
note, photo, and scratched message.

Sergeant Bill noticed my expression. "He wasn't shy about putting
them up, Jennifer."

"I never knew . . . "

At the time, I was taken aback. Only later did I realize what those notes
represented to Shawn. To him, they were the moments that mattered, and
he willingly let his brother police officers see what mattered to him.

When we went up to the front office, Renee, the business office man-
ager met us. She always had a smile and kind things to say about Shawn.
Knowing I was coming, she met me with a hug.

"Are you ready to see Shawn's desk?" she asked.

I nodded.

Shawn's cubicle looked like a shrine. It was filled with cards, flowers, notes, and photos spread out for display. I scanned the notes of condolence and stared at the photos as if I were in a history museum. There was a picture of Shawn holding an eighteen-inch-long fish while on a weekend trip with a couple of the other officers. Displayed in the corner sat a five-by-seven framed photo of Shawn in his uniform. Other photos had been on his desk from before he died—pictures of him holding Jordan and Maddi when they were born.

Next to his computer lay a piece of scratch paper with a note scrawled in pencil. It was written in Spanish in Shawn's handwriting. I drew in my breath as I read it. Quiet, Renee stood by my side.

I turned to her. "Do you know what this says?"

"No," she said. "No one around here speaks Spanish"—she smiled— "but I'd be lying if I told you we weren't curious."

"'*No hay mal, que por bien no venga*,' means 'bad will not happen unless good will come from it.'"

Of all messages!

"Renee, this is a phrase that our friends from Argentina used. But why does he have this on his desk?" I asked. "It's almost like he knew . . ."

It felt as if Shawn were talking to me himself. But as clear as his handwritten note, I knew God was speaking. *There is good in life. Good that is still worth finding. Good that is still worth living.*

God goes to great lengths to let us know he still has good things in store for our lives.

Throughout the Bible people were sent messages from God for instruction, encouragement—and healing. Jeremiah 18:1–6 is one such message:

> This is the word that came to Jeremiah from the
> LORD: "Go down to the potter's house, and there I
> will give you my message." So I went down to the
> potter's house, and I saw him working at the wheel.
> But the pot he was shaping from the clay was marred

in his hands; so the potter formed it into another pot,
shaping it as seemed best to him. Then the word of
the LORD came to me: . . . "Can I not do with you as
this potter does?" declares the Lord. "Like clay in the
hand of the potter, so are you in my hand."

God has a message for each of us to hear and live out. A message of
new work in us. The message is connected both to our moments and to
what moves us, and God chooses unique ways to speak that message. For
some, God's voice is in music, for others in reading, maybe he will speak
in a dream or through a meaningful relationship.

A message for healing that came to me strongly appeared in three
small words—*be here now*. In his creative healing wisdom, God is calling me to be present-minded. If I ignore God's message, I only avoid his
design for healing.

Our message is a gift significant not only for us, but for others:

Do not neglect your gift, which was given you
through a prophetic message. . . . Be diligent in these
matters; give yourself wholly to them, so that everyone
may see your progress. (1 Timothy 4:14–15)

The best in me is being born—moment by moment. Not because of
my loss, but because of my belief. Believing that God has good things
prepared for my life and for the days I am still granted helps me progress
and heal. Each step I take bids me to make an authentic offering of my
here and now. This is where I find healing. This is where I find something new.

The best thing we can do to promote healing is to trust. While hanging
onto God profoundly, have you ever at the same time questioned him
profusely? Have you ever surrendered everything before God, and he
appeared to look the other way? Have you ever tried to hand your life back

to God and say, "No thank you, I don't want to go through this hurt," only to hear him tell you, "You are right where you are supposed to be"?

After returning home from the police department with some of Shawn's cards and photos tucked in the side of his lunch bag, I had a fiery conversation with God.

"Okay, God, I don't know if I'll ever understand this. Why my husband? Why take Shawn in order for me to search out purpose? Why was my life created to walk without my spouse? What am I doing here? What am I going to do without him? He held me together. He made my life make sense."

And why was it that the voice inside me, that I'd come to know as God's tender speaking, seemed to be silent when I most needed to hear from him? Then I thought about my last conversation and how God placed on my heart that he was ready to help me believe. Maybe he wasn't speaking because he already had. Just as God does not waste moments, he does not waste words. Ultimately my answer is about trust—believing that God designed my life for a reason.

Whether we plan it or not, want it or not, or will decide to play along with it or not—God has a plan in mind for each of us. He is implementing that plan whether we are sad or happy. How can we be sure, though, that good will come from it? The God who is love does not fail. He is generous to comfort us in both small and big ways, and willing to lead us when we are ready to follow.

This is not to be confused with the cliché often expressed in times of loss, "Everything happens for a reason" or "This is all part of God's plan." "Shawn must have died for a reason," some may comment. No. Shawn died because one man decided to make a reckless, selfish move and take my husband's life. That is the consequence of wretched sin, not the result of God's divine plan. God grieves with us as we experience the results of living in an imperfect, sin-filled world. We can't explain away the pain by saying God must have planned it that way. God's plan isn't often obvious. In searching for words of condolence, we muddle up God's plan.

Rather than being concerned with explaining God's plan for the past, I need to believe in his purpose for the present. God's plan is not in my pain. God's plan is in my possibilities, in what I decide to do with my pain. God's plan is for me to continue living a full and vibrant life. My response is to trust—not decode, not dictate, not explain.

Like the psalmist, I searched for my path: "Show me the right path, O Lord; point out the road for me to follow. Lead me by your truth and teach me, for you are the God who saves me. All day long I put my hope in you" (Psalm 25:4–5 NLT). We don't need to know the way—God knows the road. It's our choice to follow.

Walking with God doesn't erase the grief. Walking with God strengthens us for the lasting marks of loss. I have plenty of mighty low points. Even as I write, I fear I counter my intent by making the journey sound simple or trouble-free—"Just believe and it will all work out." The truth is complicated—loss will always hurt. Maybe it will lessen or appear in varying degrees, but it won't completely disappear.

Even so, I refuse to yield to the wound, to let it cripple me. "'For I know the plans I have for you,' says the Lord. 'They are plans for good and not for disaster, to give you a future and a hope'" (Jeremiah 29:11 NLT). I set my eyes on God's promise for good.

Trusting is the most uncomfortable and frightening part of my journey. Like my steady passion for writing, God is my true constant. My freedom from debilitating pain is dependent on my response to follow God—to find where he is and walk with him. Trusting is a risk we must take if we want to allow God to create something new in us.

The second year after Shawn died, I attended a spouse's retreat hosted by C.O.P.S. (Concerns of Police Survivors), a national support group created twenty years ago for the loved ones of police officers who have died in the line of duty. The group offers recovery programming for children, families, and other individuals affected by the loss of the officer. Paul, the Minnesota chapter president, promoted the weekend until I agreed to go. He told me, "It will give you a new kind of support." I wrote in my journal:

Go up the mountain. Sit a while. Look around.
Breathe in new air. Let the breeze tickle your nose.

The sun warm your skin. Be still. Caution your heart
for what it will learn after you have reached the peak.
Stay alert. If you choose not to climb, you risk not
experiencing the highest point. Stay awake for your
best moment. Go up the mountain.

The weekend was filled with heaviness—and hope. It was a compilation of heartbreaking stories owned by eighty of the boldest women I have ever met.

One of the women at the retreat had lost her husband several years prior and is now raising four teenagers on her own. Her words stay with me as a guide: "When the hope inside of us is greater than the pain inflicted upon us, we cease to be a victim and then can say we are a survivor."

One of the most inspiring individuals I met during the retreat was C.O.P.S. executive director, Suzie Sawyer. Her mere presence emphasized her passion to assist in rebuilding the lives of surviving family members. One hug from Suzie and I felt like I mattered. I watched her dance through the weekend, offering encouragement. She's a visionary—passionately living out her mission.

A significant event for me during the weekend was a ropes course, a twenty-five to fifty foot high, tightrope jungle gym. Suzie encouraged many of the newer widows to participate in this activity, promoting it as life changing. For me it was mind-changing. Through it, I learned that the biggest obstacle keeping me from reaching for a new life was my own fear. In order to reach my goals, I had to tackle my fears, real or invented.

I was the first to volunteer for the course, which consisted of five elements. My first challenge, walk free handed across a twenty foot long inclined log. Although I wore a harness around my waist, there was nothing for me to hold on to. Psychologically, I felt there was no support at all if I fell, leaving me beyond nervous. The entire event seemed more like a dare than an afternoon pastime.

Hesitating, I stood motionless fifteen feet above the ground, grasping the pole behind me. Suzie stood below, cupping her hands to her mouth, shouting, "Jennifer, go for it! You can do this. What are you afraid of?"

My legs felt unstable. "I'm afraid of falling."

"You won't fall," she told me.

"How do you know?" I asked.

"Trust us, Jennifer. We won't let you fall."

"But . . . what if I can't do it?"

Suzie wasn't about to let me talk myself out of this. "You can do this, Jennifer. Is this the hardest thing you've ever done?"

My tears broke. I didn't want to answer but felt compelled. "No," I said.

"Is this your greatest pain or biggest challenge?" she persisted.

Tears continued. "No," I said.

"Is this your greatest fear?" she asked as if going down a list.

Tears were now streaming down my face. Why was she pushing me? "No," I whispered, loud enough for her to hear.

"You're right," she said.

I raised my eyebrows, still clenching the handhold.

"Yes, you're right," Suzie shouted. "The answer *is* no, Jennifer. I'll tell you something . . . You've already walked through your greatest hurt. This is nothing. This doesn't compare. If you've already faced your greatest fear, then what are you afraid of?"

Already in the weekend, I'd learned that *I don't know* wouldn't be accepted as an answer. "But, Suzie," I fumbled for an excuse, "I could back out of this if I wanted to. I didn't have any choice when Shawn died. I *had* to face it. I didn't *choose* to live my life without him."

My legs wobbled and my hands clutched tighter as I rationalized why it was okay for fear and hurt to keep me from accomplishing something big. Standing nearly two stories above ground, my only escape a narrow log in front of me, I gasped, "Why would I *choose* to place myself in this position?"

Suzie smiled with empathy.

"There's nothing to hold onto up here other than faith," I said. "Why would I submit myself to this craziness? I don't feel strong enough to do this."

I wanted to tell her how this was going to be. As so many times before, I wanted to be in control. Then a sudden, strong, and serene realization seized me. The voice was back, filling my senses. *Jennifer—you must* choose *your fear in order to conquer it. You must walk though your pain in order to see the other side. You have to step out confidently in faith to overcome the very thing that paralyzes you.*

This time I knew who I was talking to. *God . . . are you in this walk with me?* I couldn't stop shaking. One leg quivered like Jell-O, and I was waiting for Suzie to yell at me again to get going. As I peered down at her, though, she appeared to be waiting patiently.

God had more to say: *You run the risk of living stuck in your past and forfeiting your future if you do not* move. *You are correct. This fear, this high rope did not* choose *you. You chose it. Not because it doesn't scare you, but for the very fact it does. It is ready to conquer you with fright. But listen. You were designed to overcome. I am your strength.*

Legs shaking, arms balancing, eyes focused on the goal ahead, I thought, almost as if whispering to Shawn, *Okay . . . I'm going to do it. We crossed many streams in Honduras by foot and the trick is to jump across the stones . . . stop thinking about it and go!*

I could almost hear my husband answer me like he'd done so many times when we were together. *Let the momentum carry you. Don't hesitate. Don't look back. You will always remember. But you have to move, Jennifer. You have to do something with this.*

Suzie was watching me. Her whole body leaning forward in anticipation. *This course is not about failing; it's about trusting. Move, Jennifer. Take your first step and move. You were designed to do this.*

With trepidation and a deep breath, I let go of the pole and pressed forward. Without thinking about the security behind me, I rushed to the second station, gulping deep breaths.

Cheers erupted below, and for a moment I felt elated. Then I faced the next element—a tightrope walk across a cable.

Questions swirled in my head. "Are you sure you've got me?" I yelled to Suzie and the other women congregating below.

Back came a resounding affirmation, "We've got you! You're not going to fall." By this point they knew I needed to hear this several times. Suzie continued cheering as I inched across the cable, pointing at me, beaming at my progress. "You can do this. Look at you . . . you're doing it. Look at you!"

At the third station, I switched safety locks. My hands shook as I worked to secure myself within the harness system for the next track. Ignoring my unsteady legs, I shuffled sideways across two planks to station four and looked up in panic.

"Go up!" Suzie said.

Unnerved, I questioned, "What comes next?"

"That isn't important," she told me.

"I need to know what's ahead."

"Just take one step at a time and climb," Suzie coached. "Focus on what's directly in front of you. We'll deal with what's next when you get there."

Stay in the moment, I thought as I ascended to the fourth element, fifty feet above ground. At this height I could see what Suzie had avoided describing to me: two tightrope cords forming an extensive "X" that would force the climber's hands and feet to meet at the intersection before crossing to the other side. I couldn't imagine how I'd be able to contort my body into those narrow parameters.

It was at this point that I realized I had no plan. And maybe that was best. I simply had to take a risk—figure it out as I went along. My only other option was to quit, and that didn't seem even close to satisfying.

Holding on, my muscles tensed, I forced myself to keep moving. Even now, I'm not sure how I did it, but somehow I made it to the other side. I thought, *Just because the possibility is hidden doesn't make it impossible.*

The fifth and final station, the Spider's Web, was a net of ropes with an opening in the center. Edging out into the web, I contemplated the requirement of free-falling through the opening, allowing the pulley system to lower me to the ground. This was the last of many elements within the course that Suzie referred to as "mind over matter." She promised I could overcome anything if I determined in my mind first, regardless of fear, that I could achieve what I set out to do.

When my eyes met Suzie's, her expression told me I was already there. She had no doubt. I borrowed her faith and fell forward. This was the best part. Slowly lowering myself to the ground with the rope system, I was jubilant with my victory.

"I did it! I did it!" Like going downhill on a toboggan—I had that whooshing sensation, stimulating and reviving. I'd seen this kind of uninhibited joy many times in my little children when they accomplished a new feat. Suzie embraced me through my tears and hers.

This was triumph. I chose that day a vulnerable, unknown, frightening path—not to better understand my fear, to better understand my strength. I chose to walk through the insecurity of fright because I want to live in confidence. I choose to walk through darkness to stand on the other side of grief. Having known the pit of despair as well as having shared the depths of love, I continue to trust in a bigger adventure. God's abundant possibilities lie on the other side of what holds me back because of fear and wounded hurt. This is why I had to cross over. This is why I had to take the risk.

There's a term for the scar a horse earns in battle—"proud flesh." The wound of my loss is like the proud flesh on a horse—it is raised, it is honored, it is stronger. It is a new creation, a new part of me.

We all live with the knowledge that our days on earth are limited. It's not often acknowledged as we don't like to think about death and dying or our immortality. Still our days are numbered.

Because our time is limited, our plans, whatever they are, should be big. I am much braver since Shawn died—brave enough to make a considerable plan. It has to be big in order to stir my heart. Small plans do not inspire. There's little to no exhilaration in planning to write an e-mail. There's tremendous thrill in planning to write a book!

God created us to create, and our spirits tell us to reach farther than we dream possible. I feel my best when I am doing what he created me to do. That doesn't mean at times I don't feel intimidated. When I started to write this book, it was a big plan, comprised of many moments. I took small, halting steps.

"What is keeping you from finishing your book?" my counselor asked after many sessions.

"I don't know," I said, casting about for an acceptable answer. "What if I fail?"

"Fail in what?" she asked.

"Writing it. Selling it. Marketing it," I replied. The list in my mind was a lot longer.

"You're worrying about steps too far ahead," she told me. "You've said you find great meaning in writing. Don't let the idea of a difficult journey prevent you from actually going on it."

I sat, digesting the advice.

"What does your book look like to you?" she asked. "When it's completed, what do you see?"

"It looks comforting," I told her. "It's written to help someone else because no one should have to go through this kind of pain alone."

"That sounds like a good place to start," she replied.

So I went home and sat down at the computer.

One afternoon while cleaning my office, I ran across a folder from Shawn's college psychology class. From the notes, it appeared the professor was discussing trauma, grief, and loss.

Interesting, I thought.

Shawn had highlighted a few lines in the notebook and had written in the margins, "It's not so much what happens to people, but what they come to believe about it and make of it."

These words in my husband's handwriting struck me deep—in how many more ways would God outline my map for healing? Further down the page, Shawn had scribbled, "What is God doing here, and how, and why?" Shawn's words provided for me a new connection with him, his questions becoming my questions—What? How? Why?

We are on a lifelong journey that will be filled with questions. More important will be the beliefs we form around those questions. What will we make of our loss? What will happen if we commit to loving generously, giving graciously, and trusting wholeheartedly?

I believe genuine healing will occur.

God is using my circumstance as well as my talents to create something new. He can see my potential when all I can see is tragedy. I am both his wounded child and as his masterpiece. God has a brand new composition in mind for each of us. God works to reshape me—encouraging me to live boldly.

Following God's plan—to give, to trust, and to love—brings new life in the midst of pain. It can't be both ways. Either we live fully or we don't. Either we are alive or we are dead to life. Either we believe in God or we deny him. Either we live out our purpose or we are not living on purpose. One way is life-giving. The other is life-stealing. It would be easy to choose the life-draining choice, but God's purpose isn't in our hurt; his purpose is in our living.

God calls us to participate in life, not to be mere spectators. Life is made by creating. Life is sustained by creating. Life is upheld and inspired by creating. God calls us to dream, desire, envision, invent, consider, explore, converse, discover, love, and believe in a life larger than we can imagine.

I cling to creating something new each day. It doesn't matter what we create—if we knit a sweater, change the oil in the car, or paint like van Gogh—the important piece is to do something outside of ourselves with the passion inside of us. We discover more—about ourselves, the world around us, and the God we follow—by creating than in any other way.

I feel closest to God when I am creating something new. Why? Because God created us to create. When we make something new in our lives, God is also crafting something new *inside* of us. In the midst of creating, I am fulfilled and can say, "I made a difference."

I have found that the best therapy for loss is to do something with the grief. Nearly anything is better than nothing. Of course, I am speaking of healthy, life-promoting activities, not abusive addictions such as alcohol abuse, drug use, overeating, obsessive shopping, and so on. And the idea to *do something* should not be confused with an overcommitted schedule. Anything done in excess can have adverse effects on our overall health.

Two summers after Shawn died I planted an herb garden with a variety of greens in front of my house. With some expenditure of time, emotion, and effort, I cared for my box-garden every day with watering, tending, and weeding. My very first salad from what I'd grown tasted fresh and healthy and extremely satisfying. When I extend myself into an activity that promotes energy and well being, I'm rejuvenated and feel a sense of satisfaction, which has a healing touch.

Philippians 2:12–13 says, "Keep it up. Better yet, redouble your efforts. Be energetic in your life of salvation, reverent and sensitive before God. That energy is God's energy, an energy deep within you" (MSG). Through his Spirit, God places the potential for healing inside of us. It's up to us to use God's energy.

Healing is work. God's Spirit works healing in us when we work to heal. I don't want to miss my life. I want to live it. My best writing comes from my most inconsolable days. I will use what I have and work with it. I am going to take the advantage.

Anything where we must exert a part of ourselves will bring benefits. We need to move, keep going, stay focused, be present-minded and allow ourselves to experience the enjoyment of engaging with life.

"To all who mourn . . . he will give a crown of beauty for ashes, a joyous blessing instead of mourning, festive praise instead of despair" (Isaiah 61:3 NLT). Through what we create, we affirm our belief in God's work. We take part in praise of him for something new. We acknowledge that life has both blessing and meaning.

Our *doing something* needs to be intentional. Every day provides the opportunity to make a change. It can be as simple as making a cup of coffee or as elaborate as leading a support group. Do something. Try something. Do try.

Months after Shawn died I met with Father Reiser, seeking some level of understanding from this white-haired priest's wisdom. I listened closely as he spoke, this man who had such influence on both Shawn's and my spiritual journeys in pursuing a relationship with Christ.

"You will not believe me now, Jennifer," Father Reiser told me, "but come find me in heaven and let me know if I'm right. I trust you will thank God for every day following September sixth, two thousand five—as each day will be more splendid than the day preceding it."

I looked at this seasoned priest—whom I admired and respected—feeling both skepticism and awe. What could he possibly mean?

He continued, "It will be in these days that you come to know God more fully than ever before, as will many others, from Shawn's sacrifice."

"It's the hardest thing I've ever done," I said.

"I know," he said, slowly rocking his head, his eyes almost shut in reflection. His tone held absolute certainty. "You can't see now what you will see then—inside the tragedy God is working wonders."

I didn't want to believe there could be anything wonderful in Shawn's dying. And, in truth, there wasn't anything wonderful in the fact that Shawn died. Still, the message stirred my heart, and what was wonderful is how deeply Shawn's life touched my own and that of countless others. Like a friend expressed in an e-mail, "Shawn's life encourages me to live less selfishly and love more blindly." This has become my desire as well—to live and love deeper.

The last morning I was with Shawn, he kissed me like he would never see me again. I was running a quick errand to develop film, and he raced out to the garage to kiss me through the rolled-down car window. I told him I'd be home for lunch so we could eat together before he had to leave for work.

"Bye, honey. I love you," he said, cupping my face in his hands.

"I love you too," I told him, amused. "You're goofy—I'm only going to the store."

Hours later I saw Shawn in the ambulance. All that mattered at the moment of his death was how he had lived and loved—that he experienced the life his Creator designed for him, that his heart knew and loved God and that he had shared this love with others.

What did my life look like outside of that ambulance? What do I make with the twenty-four hours of each day in front of me? I believe I remain in this life to add meaning—if even in small ways. To wave and smile at my elderly neighbor who lives across the street or to wait patiently in line at the store or to take an extra second or two to listen to what my children are really trying to tell me.

God is on a mission for us to know the extent of his love—to catch a glimpse of how deep and wide, long and high is the love of Christ (Ephesians 3:18–19). In him our longing will be made complete. Am I ready to accept his love into my life?

God also wants us to set our sight on what really matters. "We fix our eyes not on what is seen, but on what is unseen. For what is seen is temporary, but what is unseen is eternal" (2 Corinthians 4:18). We waste much energy and emotion on regrets or worries that will make no difference in eternity. I do not want to waste my life on temporary things.

Life is precious and fragile and fleeting. No discomfort, no small or large irritation, no misinterpretation, no silly dispute or made-up worry compares to the tremendous pain of loss. Once someone we love is gone, we are left begging for more time, more discussion, more interactions, and more chances to love. We bargain for more moments. So we must place our energy on loving those people who fill our lives *now*.

Will I embrace the gift of this moment? Will I live less selfishly and love more deeply? Will I take the minute in front of me and walk inside those sixty seconds to live the importance of today?

I don't want to settle for an unfulfilling life because I lack the courage to go after the life I really want. This is what matters to me.

What does a typical day look like? There is no typical. I am not looking for a normal life—I am in search of a content one.

Like taking a random summer day while my kids are prowling in the pantry for breakfast and announcing, "It's beach day!" We make an impromptu picnic with odds and ends from the refrigerator and set out to enjoy our free day together.

Sitting on an oversized beach towel we snack on carrot sticks and pea pods. Jordan grabs a handful of peanuts and starts shelling them one by one. With ocean-blue eyes that hold extra glimmer from the reflection of the sun, Jordan peers at me as if he can read my mind and asks, "Do I look like my dad?"

"Yes," I say, watching his tender grin.

"Mom," he tells me. "I feel 'licorice-y and pop-lar-ishy'"

I raise my eyebrows. I need interpretation.

"Like licorice and lollipops," he says.

"Oh," I reply as if it all makes sense. "And how does that feel?"

"It feels like you are eating a lollipop," he tells me. "It feels good."

I nod as Maddi grabs my elbow.

"Mom, when we done eating, we go swimming?" she asks with eyes that look *pop-lar-ishy*. "That's an idea, Mom!"

"Oh, yes, Miss Maddi," I tell her. "That certainly is an idea! A very *good* idea."

Looking over his shoulder, Jordan is talking in a soft voice.

"Why did you die?" he asks. "Oh, a car killed you?"

"You talking to God, Jo-dan?" Madelynn asks her brother.

Jordan replies, "No, I'm talking to my dad."

Then feigning a coarse cough he says, "I'm gonna burp!"

Both my son and daughter snicker.

Turning his head, Jordan asks, "Dad—did that make you laugh?"

I chuckle, certain Shawn would find humor in our children's silliness.

Looking back at me, Jordan wants to know, "Did Dad whistle?"

"Yes, he was good at whistling."

"Can you whistle?" Jordan asks.

"A little." I try to demonstrate, but my failed attempt leaves me laughing as I admit, "Barely."

Madelynn wants to be a part of the interaction and says, "Me have to tell my daddy something."

"Okay," Jordan tells her by way of permission.

"Why you killed?" Madelynn asks, looking past us both at the navy-blue lake, her voice light and affectionate.

Either unaware or pretending her conversation isn't one-sided, she uses short pauses as if on the telephone, "Oh . . . you killed? A car? Oh . . . okay, Daddy. I love you . . . goodbye. We go swimming, Daddy."

Eager to swim, my children grab their goggles and tell me they want to snorkel.

And that was our moment. Moving. Doing something. Incorporating our loss. Not being constrained by time. Encouraging each other. Loving one another. Embracing the now. Choosing contentment. Creating something new with the day.

These are how our days go—moment by moment. Not always carefree, often presenting challenges—but still making an effort.

Even when I'm scared, sad, or disappointed, I still have great things to offer within those moments. I can be who I was designed to be, trusting God is with me. This is my small offering. I share a part of me and it helps. Each exchange of love makes a difference. *If I could sing to you, I would sing with my best voice.*

And whatever I create in those moments is the testament of my life—one that hopes to humbly gravitate toward God, keep moving with the inclines, work through hurts, live with intention, be engaged with those I love, and captivated by those who love me.

Because God made us for now.

Until I cross that barrier of time—*I believe.*

In my heart's memory of Shawn Barrington Silvera
March 7, 1973—September 6, 2005

Acknowledgments

I am in the vast countryside of Sunderland, Canada. It's a chilly October morning and I have just come in from running. The deep violet verbenas line the walkway up to the house where I am staying—a place that brings me full circle.

It is here we took our last vacation together two weeks before Shawn died. We made the fifteen-hour road trip with our children and Shawn's mom, stopping along the way to eat fudge, watch Jordan chase seagulls, diaper-change Madelynn. No rushing. No strict schedule. Visiting relatives. Enjoying each other.

I could never have predicted that I'd return three years later with a book completed and my husband's life ended. And even though my heart is heavy with his absence, my spirit is appreciative for all my life's interactions and immeasurable blessings. Life is short. Life is fragile. And life is very blessed.

To my family and friends, thank you for blessing my life.

Jordan and Madelynn—*Vidas de mi vida!* I write because of you. You are my eyes, my heart, my brightest ideas—my life. I adore our time together. Always know I love you with every part of me.

Deanna—You have carried my burden as if it were your own. I'm indebted to you for not giving up on me. You are the purest friend I know.

Cynthia—You accept me on any day at any time exactly as I am. You let me feel every part of this story without apology or judgment. How rare to find my best friends in my sisters.

Mom and Dad (Gamma and Papa)—You raised me to treasure life, family, and dreams. You raised me to stand in confidence and faith. I can believe stronger because of how you love me. My children are stronger by how you love them.

Adam and Lori, my kind-hearted brother and his wife—Thank you for your sensitive care in my life. Thank you for taking my kids to the park, weekly phone calls, and music to inspire my writing.

Sarah, my little sister—Thank you for taking care of me in meaningful ways—loving my kids, flat-ironing my hair, programming my cell phone. Making me laugh when I need it most.

Bonnie, my mother-in-law—We are kindred spirits. Your loss is my loss and your heart is my heart. I am so glad Shawn connected us in this life.

To Shawn's family: Mark, Deanne, Natalie, Henry, Nicole, Nick, Joshua, Zackary, Anna, Uncle Herman, Auntie Pat, Uncle John, Aunt Kathy, Brian, Aimee, Cameron, and Jennifer (faithful friend)—Thank you for continuing to walk in our lives, for loving us and letting us know we will always be a part of you.

Andrea and Ben—From Web site design, to long chats, to tears and then more tears, you have never ceased to help me see not only the beauty in my loss but the beauty in my life.

Cindy and Megan—Thank you for making sure I'm never alone, letting me know I'm stronger than I think, and eating red-velvet cake with me on my birthday!

Sarah J.—Thank you for every midnight visit and late night run. For being impressed with me when I feel defeated. For eating my salads and enjoying simple things. Mostly for reminding me we have good lives.

Dana—I love that we share such similar visions in life. You read my mind! May God guide our creative inspirations for his great work.

Karissa—Your touch on my life is unwavering. You have taught me how to wake up each morning and welcome health and strength into my day. Thank you for the countless hours of watching my kids.

Tracie, my parent coach and speaking companion—You encourage me to see the possibilities that easily hide themselves. One meeting with you and I am ready to try again and again.

Lisa—I love our talks while on the elliptical machines! Thank you for letting me borrow your eyes through your stunning photography. I know you understand the many layers of my gratitude.

Chanttel, my mentor—You have gone before me, heartening me to be a courageous fighter, strong mother, long-lasting friend, and above all a believer. Welcome to our strange normal.

Carrie—I hurt with you in your loss and am blessed to have someone who understands the depth of where we've been.

Sue M. and Yvette, women of God—my prayer warriors—Thank you for covering my life.

Jeremy and Cindy—Every discussion with you leads me to my next step on this journey and teaches me to own my story. I love you both.

Paul and Lisa & the Lifeteen band—Sharing our music together is the most soothing time of my entire week. Thank you for letting me come, turn off my mind for a few hours, and simply sing.

Kristen, Ericka, and the Be Here Now committee—Thank you for your tremendous response to my grieving heart and for helping me create, design, and accomplish meaningful new things in my life.

Pat—Thank you for your grace-filled hugs on Sundays.

Sue J.—You have a magical way of reading my heart. Thank you for getting it. Thank you for being there.

Jeannie—Thank you for helping me package my ideas until I was convinced to strive for more.

Liza—You are a bright smile in my life.

My wonderful neighbors—Jamy and Julie, thank you for watching out for me. Beth, thanks for walks around the block. Kelty, you make my favorite apple crisp. Bob, thanks for playing cribbage and reminding me when it is garbage day.

Jami, my lifelong friend—Your influence in my life has been a key to my book writing. There hasn't been a day I haven't thought about our friendship. I will always love you.

Sergeant Bill—Thank you for walking with us from the earliest moments of loss . . . and for the hundreds of times you have told me that you will always be there and that we are never a bother.

Steve W.—Thank you for the countless times you have fixed something at our house or brought M&Ms! No words could speak stronger for how much you care or for how much we appreciate you.

Renee—You are the heart that accomplishes what I have left undone. Thank you for filling in the gaps.

City of Lino Lakes, LLPD, and LEMA—Thank you for your tremendous response and assistance after Shawn died.

To the First Responderes and all those who guard the Thin Blue Line—Thank you for your dedication and service.

Suzie S., Paul G., and C.O.P.S.—Thank you for showing me how to conquer my self-invented fears so that I could live brave.

Jan—Your spiritual direction has been my constant breathing space since Shawn died. Here I find comfort, safety, and new ways to live out my purpose.

Jina—This book would not exist without your sight to see beyond the idea. Working with you brought clarity and confidence, an ultimate piece of my healing.

Belen (Néna)—Your year with us was invaluable to me. *Gracias por todo tu amor y ayuda.* My kids still call the guest room "Néna's Room."

Ruth, Rafa, and the Mayorga family—To my Honduran girlfriend who eats chocolate! You are my other family. *Dios nos bendiga.*

The Galindo family—Thank you for providing us a home in Honduras. Doña Aminta is never forgotten.

Laura and Jorge—Thank you for giving Shawn his second name, Miguel. I can't wait to drink hot cocoa with cream again! *Siempre amigos.*

Each nanny—My gratitude for the care you gave to my tenderhearts when I was at work on this book.

Kayla—Every ounce of love you give is multiplied.

Mike, Mary, Danny, David, and Emily—Each visit to the farm is a time to rest, explore, run free, and feel completely cared for and loved.

Uncle Bob, Kristine, and the Dorn family—Family ties unite us, loss changes us, and love connects us.

Grandma & Grandpa Vander Poel and Grandma & Grandpa Dorn—You are always in my heart.

Jim, Ashlyn, Evan, Ian—A weekend at your house is better than Disney World! Thanks for being a vibrant part of Jordan's and Maddi's lives.

In memory of Aunt Peggy and my loving friend Mary Jo—Your

lives are measured by the love you shared. I am thankful you shared your love with me.

In memory of all fallen officers who made the ultimate sacrifice.

Kodiak Coffee, Starbucks, and Hardwater Creek Library of Forest Lake, MN—All my favorite places to write, usually with a cup of decaf coffee and cream. To the coffee baristas, thank you for every time you asked about my book.

Dawn—Thank you for the stunning jewelry design!

Erin—Thank you for your gift of music.

Mitch, Clay, and Sarah—Thank you for keeping my best interest at heart.

Dr. Amatuzio—Thank you for taking compassionate care of Shawn.

Roberts Family Funeral Home—Thank you for serving my family in its most critical hour with honor, integrity, and the finest details.

Father Reiser—You have shaped my faith. From the time I was a teenager you told me, "If God is leading you, how can you say no?" Thank you for helping me answer my call.

To my editors—Susan, Jon, Paulette, and Dawn—Thank you for risking, questioning, and driving me through every rewrite to press closer and clearer to the heart of the message.

To my publisher, Dennis—Thank you for taking a leap with my book, for believing in me so that I could again believe in myself.

To the marketing team at Kregel, especially Cat—Thank you!

Proverbs 31 Ministries—Thank you for your foresight, insight, and godly sight to help women like myself reach out with the talents we are given to experience a greater reality of God in our lives.

Shawn, cute boy—I loved you since I was seventeen. Your love inspired me to create my best work. I am made better for each moment our lives walked this earth together. You were made for me.

Loving God—You see the whole story. I offer this book, my best, to you. Thank you for introducing me to love, sustaining me by love, and helping me believe all things are possible by your grace and love.

To my readers—In your own journeys of brokenness, whatever shape that takes, I pray that God will bring you back to a life of hope and healing. I am humbled to walk a small step of the path with you.

May God's grace open each of us to what matters as we seek and find lives filled with depth and love. I pray you find much meaning along the way. For more information about my ministry, please visit http://www.believenow.com.